BIOGRAPHY
FULLSTONE
(NEVADA)

D0787856

DR. MARY

Mary H Fulstone

DR. MARY

The Story of Mary Hill Fulstone, M.D.
A Nevada Pioneer

By

Dixie Westergard

Jack Bacon & Company
Reno, Nevada
2004

DUST JACKET PHOTO: Children's Hospital, San Francisco, California,
with recovering children and hospital staff on the sun roof, 1917.
Special Collections University of California Berkeley (Call # 1989.058 1:25).

Jack Bacon & Company
516 South Virginia Street
Reno, Nevada

www.JackBacon.com

FIRST EDITION

For The
"Dr. Mary Babies"

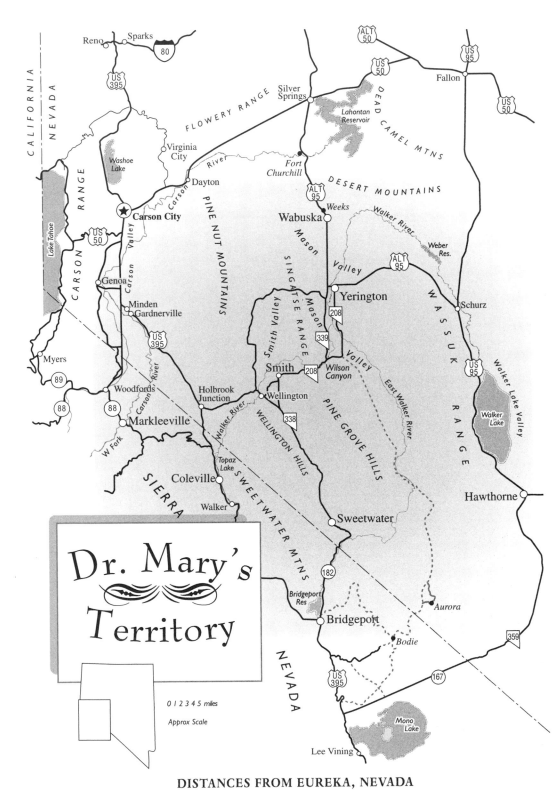

DISTANCES FROM EUREKA, NEVADA

Elko – 113 miles • Reno – 242 miles • Carson City – 242 miles

TABLE OF CONTENTS

PROFESSIONALISM

In recent years, fast food restaurants have redefined the family evening meal and moved it from the home to the automobile or a line in front of a counter. Other profound family changes have occurred as a result of single parent families or two working parents.

Christian churches in America have changed their style and even some concepts-sexual orientation for example-to meet the needs of their parishioners. Lawyers and society have changed the legal climate so that not only is it the right of every citizen to sue but to do so means we are not responsible for our actions. Even the practice of medicine has changed as Congress legalized abortion, prohibited professional courtesy because it induces "kickbacks," and established medical practice as a business. In a world that is rapidly changing, family and community values, ethics, and the professions are under assault.

In earlier times, it was commonly thought that there were only three professions: medicine, law, and clergy. The late Supreme Court Justice Louis D. Brandeis said it best when he stated in the early 1900s that a profession has three characteristics:

First. A profession is an occupation for which the necessary preliminary training is intellectual in character, involving knowledge and to some extent learning, as distinguished from mere skill.

Second. It is an occupation which is pursued largely for others and not merely for one's self.

Third. It is an occupation in which the amount of financial return is not the accepted measure of success.

In the twenty-first century, do all of the above three professions hold up to this standard, and do they have exclusive right to the title profession? Are there other occupations that meet these criteria? I will let the reader answer the first question, but the answer to the second is "no." Being a nurse or a teacher involves learning, is done for others, and financial reward is not an incentive or a measure of success.

Although Brandeis' axiom defines a profession, it does not go far enough to define the practice of medicine. To administer healing to those in need is much greater than the sum of knowledge, altruism, and service over proprietary reward. Medicine can only exist with a responsible ethical code that ensures public trust. Quality of service, duty to the patient and the community, honor, and integrity are absolutely necessary for good medical care. Just as important is the doctor's responsibility for colleagues' actions. We cannot allow one doctor to harm a patient regardless of whether it is due to neglect, emotional or physical impairment, or lack of knowledge.

Traditionally the skills necessary to practice medicine are acquired through postgraduate training utilizing a preceptor or mentor who demonstrates the skill, the art, and the wisdom of practice. In my forty years since medical school, I have seen no one who embodies the professionalism of medicine more than Dr. Mary. She has been a mentor for the students of Smith Valley, such as Dr. Robin Titus, who have followed her leadership and example. She not only has served her patients with the core values of compassion, dedication, and personal sacrifice, but has served her community and state with dignity and excellence.

In her biography of Dr. Mary Fulstone, Dixie Westergard, has done an excellent job of documenting the various ways that Dr. Mary touched the lives of so many citizens of Nevada. Also, many doctors, some of whom have added comments, have observed on a collegial level how she was respected in the profession and exemplified professionalism. In this changing world, one thing stands high that has not changed, and that is that medicine is a most noble profession, and Dr. Mary is an outstanding example of what medicine is about.

Anton P. Sohn, M.D., FASCP
Professor and Chairman, Dept. Path.
Director, History of Medicine Program
University of Nevada School of Medicine

"Dr. Mary practiced medicine
longer than any other doctor in Nevada."

Smith Valley Bed and Breakfast Brochure

INTRODUCTION

Most older Nevadans have heard about Dr. Mary Fulstone. Many northern Nevadans knew her well. And, rural Nevadans in Mason Valley and Smith Valley depended on Dr. Mary as a physician from the 1920s until the 1980s.

For sixty years Dr. Mary tended to the medical needs of three generations of ranchers, miners, Northern Paiutes, and their families. She home delivered over 4,000 babies and became a legend in her own time; admired by people far away as well as nearby.

Still healthy during her 80s, Dr. Mary delivered Kimber Lee, her own great-granddaughter.

Until her death in 1987, Dr. Mary's large ranch house served as her family home and medical office. Now the house is open to visitors as a welcoming Bed and Breakfast. The location, the size, and especially the rooms of the house help tell the story of Dr. Mary Fulstone - wife, mother, rural doctor, and community leader.

A visitor opening the front door enters a world of framed 1960s and 1970s newspaper clippings on the fireplace mantle and family photographs smiling from everywhere. The enormity of Dr. Mary's life unfolds from the newspaper reviews.

Somehow Mary Ruth Hill combined all of her dreams into reality. Her zest for life and robust health acted as allies which paved the way. A fun-loving sense of humor carried her through hard times.

The purpose of this biography is to honor Native Nevadan, Mary Hill Fulstone, M.D., and to learn from her remarkable life.

It seems as though "Dr. Mary" designed puzzle pieces for her life, then put the pieces together through her 95 years. Her puzzle fit together snugly, brilliantly just as her exemplary life did.

Dr. Mary's Puzzle Pieces:

Childhood
Higher Education
Family and Friends
Medical Career – 60 years
Bureau of Indian Affairs Contract
State Board of Education – 19 years
Smith Valley School Board – 24 years
Soroptomist International and other social groups

TIME LINE – MARY HILL FULSTONE, M.D.

1892	- Mary Ruth Hill born in Eureka, Nevada
1896	- John Hill, Mary's father, moved his family to Carson City, Nevada (Ella, wife; Jenny and Mary, daughters)
1896	- Arlington Hotel - Hill family business and home
1900 - 1907	- North Ward Elementary School, Carson City, Nevada
1907 - 1911	- Carson City High School
1911 - 1915	- University of California at Berkeley, B.A. Degree
1915 - 1917	- University of California at San Francisco - Medical School
1918 - 1920	- Medical Internship; Children's Hospital and San Francisco County Hospital
1919	- Mary Hill and Fred Fulstone married
1920 - 1985	- Mary Hill Fulstone, M.D. practiced medicine in Smith Valley and Yerington, Nevada - delivered over 4,000 babies
1920s	- Fulstone Children: Fred, David, Richard, Eleanor and Jeanne (twins)
1954	- Lyon County Hospital - Dr. Mary influenced its building
1954	- Organized Courtesy Staff for Lyon County Medical Center
1930s - 1950s	- Board Member of Smith Valley School Board - 24 years
1957 - 1976	- State Board of Education - 19 years
1970s	- Chief of Staff for Lyon Health Center
1980s	- Eyesight failing; at 88 years delivered Kimber Lee, her great-granddaughter
1950 to Present	- Awards and honors for Dr. Mary
1987	- Mary Fulstone, M.D. died at age 95

CHAPTER ONE

CHILDHOOD

Mary Ruth Hill was born in 1892 in the small mining town of Eureka, Nevada. Her father, John Nelson Hill, from Canada, became a naturalized citizen in 1874. John Hill worked as an accountant for the Eureka and Palisade Railroad. Eventually he became the manager for the station.

Her mother, Ella Riley Hill, originally from the Midwest, came out to San Jose Normal School to prepare to teach school. She worked before and after marrying John Hill, even though it was unusual for a woman to teach after marriage in the late 1800s.

Most of the Eureka homes had only one or two rooms. These plain wooden structures were without paint or landscaping. They had been built quickly when the silver boom began. A smell of wood, burning down to charcoal for the smelters, hovered overhead.

John Hill must have decided that mining was not stable and neither was railroading in Eureka, since it depended on iron and ore from the mines to make a profit.

Perhaps, not surprisingly, a cautious Canadian, Mary Hill's father, accepted the position of accountant at the Nevada State Prison in Carson City. He set up the first books for the prison.

Not long after the Hills moved to Carson City, a flood tore

the Eureka trestle bridge apart. Later a fire burned more of the trestles, and then the national economy crashed. The Eureka Palisade Railroad could not recover. *Nevada Bicentennial Book*

The Eureka and Palisade Railroad hauled ore out and carried in supplies. *Nevada Official Bicentennial Book*. Its friendly whistle must have been a welcome sound to Mary and her friends in this remote town.

When Mary's father took an accounting job with the Nevada State Prison, her family moved to Carson City, a small state capital at only 3,000 people. Four-year old Mary did not want to leave her Eureka playmates, especially the Kind children, who seemed like part of her family.

Horses pulled buggies and stagecoaches full of passengers into Carson City. Sometimes a pedestrian had to choose between stepping in a horse paddy or a mud puddle.

This fairy tale capitol had no indoor plumbing, only out-houses. There was no running water and no electricity. Carson City offered inaugural balls, but few comforts. *Nevada Bicentennial Book*

The elegant Capitol building in Carson City stood tall and proud. It told the citizens that Nevada was now a state in the Union. Officials met and passed laws.

Carson City school children like Mary visited the legislature then, as now.

A primitive lifestyle existed inside the fairy tale beauty of streets lined with painted houses, trees, flowers and fancy fences. Streets in Carson City were wet, muddy and messy in the winter. They were dusty and full of potholes the rest of the year.

In the 1890s Mary Hill and other children had few toys so they made their own games. The summer concerts on the Capitol grounds provided opportunities for childhood fun. Adults relaxed and listened to the music while the young ones played hide-and-seek, tag or ran races.

Being with friends provided the best kind of entertainment for Mary. She played little girl games with Elsie Farrar and the Brougher sisters. She went shopping with her friend, Mrs. Jim Butler (Belle) of Tonopah mining fame and fortune, and Mary helped Miss Theresa Smith, her pretty North Ward elementary school teacher, as often as possible.

The Hill family moved into the Arlington Hotel on Main Street when Mary's father and a partner leased it. The hotel had a fine Chinese cook. He liked Mary and her friends and fed them tasty samples when they popped into his kitchen.

Mary liked to read for another kind of fun. She and her older sister, Jenny, chose as many books on library day as they could carry. They hid their bedroom light by putting a blanket over the door transom (the window at the top of the door), so they could read as late as they wanted without their parents knowing.

Mary, Jenny and the other older school children went to the public Saturday night dances. There were no school dances because of religious convictions. Curfew at the public dances was midnight and not a minute later - a rule strictly enforced by parents and church ministers.

Mary also enjoyed playing basketball. To this day a large photograph of Mary Hill with her

One Room School

Dr. Mary attended the North Ward Elementary School in Carson City. It was a typical one room school. One teacher taught all ages and classes – 1 to 8. Books, paper, pencils, crayons, rulers and any other needed supplies were purchased by parents. Books were wrapped to keep them clean. The opening of school was around September 15th. By May 10th school was out, since the farm boys were needed at home. A failure meant staying in the same class another year. Discipline was not a problem, because parents took a misbehaving child "to the woodshed". Punishment was to remind the child that he was sent to school to learn.

A large blackboard hung on one wall of the room. Students in good standing were allowed to remain after school and help teacher clean the blackboard and erasers for the next day. Older boys brought in firewood for the pot belly stove. The privies were down a cold walk at the back of the yard.

The curriculum had all the basics of reading, writing, spelling, arithmetic, geography, and history. It also included topics on patriotism, saluting the flag, and saying the Pledge of Allegiance and singing "America."
Nevada Official Bicentennial Book.

Championship Carson High School basketball team greets visitors at the bottom of the ranch house staircase. Her eyes sparkle with a bit of mischief, and her smile softens your thoughts about the world. Her long, brown hair was pulled back stylishly.

Mary kept busy with school, team sports, Loyalty Club (which had projects like the Y.W.C.A.), the Episcopal church and summer camping trips to Glenbrook, Lake Tahoe. One year W. J. Hunting, the Carson High School principal, and the girls' basketball coach, took the team to Tonopah and Goldfield. After traveling on the night train they played league basketball games all day.

One summer, Mary and about eight of her high school friends planned a camping trip to Lake Tahoe. They were in good condition and walked up King's Canyon and Spooner to the Lake. Mrs. Amy Yerington chaperoned the first week of the trip. She arranged for the girls to stay at the Bliss House at Glenbrook for a few nights. The girls ate well during their outing because their mothers sent wonderful food to them by stagecoach each evening.

After swimming, hiking, and camping, Mary and her friends used most of their money for a boat ride on a glass-bottom steamer that went around Lake Tahoe. When the steamer stopped at a campground, the girls explored and met other campers. At Bijou they joined in the fun around a bonfire and camped overnight. They considered the boat ride the highlight of their stay at Lake Tahoe. These strong, healthy, and enthusiastic girls walked home to Carson City at the end of the third week and began planning their next camping trip to Lake Tahoe.

Mary graduated from Carson High School with a class of eleven students in 1911. She followed the lead of her favorite math teacher, Helen Chartz. Miss Chartz graduated from the University of California, Berkeley and encouraged Mary to go there, too, because of her strong mathematics skills. Mary expected to work harder in English classes since her writing needed improvement, and she did.

CHAPTER TWO

UNIVERSITY OF CALIFORNIA, BERKELEY, BACHELOR OF ARTS

UNIVERSITY OF CALIFORNIA, SAN FRANCISCO, MEDICAL SCHOOL

Mary Hill went to the University of California, Berkeley in 1911. There were 1,000 students in her freshman class, and she lived in College Hall the first year. She majored in math and planned to teach school. But, she liked the sciences best and took all the science classes she could. The pre-med students in these courses became special friends. Their excitement about medicine, along with their encouragement, pulled her toward a medical career.

University Science Classes

At Berkeley Mary Hill liked the science classes best. Some of the science classes:

Biology – the science of life or living matter in all its forms; origin, growth, reproduction;

Human anatomy – the science of the structure of animals; dissection for study of structure;

Chemistry – the science that investigates the composition of substances;

Physics – the science dealing with natural laws and processes;

Physiology – the science dealing with the functions of living

Organisms – the body, its systems;

Zoology – the science concerning the structure and functions of animals;

Psychology – the science of mind or of mental states and processes;

The science of human nature and behavior;

Kinesiology – the science of motion in man;

Organic chemistry – the science that investigates the composition of living organisms.

NOTE: Laboratory classes were required with many of the sciences. "Labs" provided opportunities for hands on experimentation and observation in the class work.

Stories of Dr. Eliza Cook of nearby Carson Valley may have helped to inspire Mary to pursue a career in medicine. Dr. Cook had a reputation for fine caring ways. And, her famous horse and buggy driving from patient to patient, even in snow and ice, was a common topic of praise. Dr. Cook practiced medicine locally from 1884 to 1921.

Mary decided to be a doctor in a time when only a few women like Dr. Eliza Cook entered the medical field except as nurses. Surprisingly, Mary's parents supported her decision to study medicine, even though Carson City's Dr. Donald Maclean strongly urged her not to seek such a difficult and demanding path in life! A faint-hearted young woman would not pursue a degree in medicine in the year 1915.

Getting accepted to a predominantly man's medical program was extremely difficult, and if accepted, class competition would be fierce. But, Mary did not have a faint heart. Challenge and competition did not frighten this young lady. It inspired her.

Mary Hill did her student internship at the San Francisco County Hospital and at Children's Hospital, San Francisco, California. Dr. Elizabeth Keyes, Chief of Obstetrics at Children's Hospital, had a great influence on Mary. Dr. Keyes took Mary and the other three girls in the class of 34 with her on home baby deliveries. These house calls gave them valuable first-hand experience. It was perfect preparation for a future rural doctor with no hospital...perfect preparation for Mary Hill.

The flu epidemic of 1918 came to San Francisco when Mary Hill was interning at Children's Hospital. Doctors, interns, and nurses worked long hours to keep patients alive, but no medicines existed to cure the flu symptoms. Only rest, mustard plasters, and steam inhalators could be offered. (A mustard plaster was made of powdered mustard, moistened in a cloth, then placed on the chest). Many died in this terrible time. One day during the epidemic Mary looked at another intern and wondered out loud what she looked like under the mask she always wore. This silly remark made everyone laugh. A good laugh helped to relieve some of the tension of the sad flu epidemic. *Oral History.*

The *Reno Gazette-Journal* recently carried this vivid account of the 1918 flu epidemic. It helps us understand what Dr. Mary dealt with in her medical internship.

In 1957 the Asian flu killed an estimated 70,000 Americans, and the so-called Spanish flu of 1918 claimed the lives of more than half a million people in the United States. Although strangely forgotten by most Americans, the Spanish flu pandemic has been the subject of literature (notably Katherine Anne Porter's "Pale Horse, Pale Rider") and of intense, but previously fruitless, medical study.

The Spanish flu erupted overnight and wiped out entire villages at opposite ends of the Earth, depressing the world's population for 10 years. It was much more virulent than any flu since – one could wake up healthy and be dead by nightfall.

What kind of flu killed young U.S. servicemen fighting World War I within a single day?

The worldwide influenza epidemic reached Chicago in September 1918, and in the next eight weeks more than 8,500 deaths were recorded from influenza and pneumonia – double the normal death rate from all causes.

The epidemic was different from all others, preying heavily

on people 20 to 40 years old, normally the most resistant group. Nurses found themselves fighting raging fevers and delirium, profuse nose bleeds and lungs filling with fluid that drowned the victims in their own fluids.

Mary did not crumble under the deathly flu epidemic. Her endurance and love of medicine were a mighty pair.

While interning at Children's Hospital Mary worked in the infectious disease ward. She shared this incident in her Oral History:

> I remember as a child growing up my mother was so afraid I'd get sick or get something that she was very careful with us. And if somebody was sick, she'd make us walk around the block instead of pass the house for fear we'd catch something. So she came when I was an intern at Children's Hospital; she came down to visit me. She was in my room while I was working. I was on communicable diseases [rotation]. And they phoned down to the room and said, "Is Dr. Hill there"?
>
> And she said, "No, she's out."
>
> "Well, tell her that there's a diphtheria case that's just come in and for her to come right over."
>
> And my mother said, "Oh, but Mary's never had diphtheria." So that was really the joke of the hospital. If anyone'd come in with anything they'd say, "Well, oh, Mary, have you had this?" [Laughs]

Dr. Mary talked of her medical school instructors with high praise and respect. She remembered their skills and personalities vividly and enjoyed talking about them. One instructor, Dr. Saxton Pope, operated on her mother for a ruptured gall bladder. He had fine surgical techniques and a wonderful way with patients. But, she always made it clear that Dr. Elizabeth Keyes, Head of Obstetrics at Children's Hospital, influenced her the most.

The interns rotated services at Children's Hospital so they would have background in each area: three months in children, three months in surgery, three months in obstetrics, three months in anesthesia and laboratory.

On her way to completing her M.D. program, Mary Hill visited her sister, Jenny, who was teaching school in Smith Valley, Nevada. There Mary found and fell in love with Fred Fulstone, a hardy, handsome Smith Valley rancher.

Fred Fulstone came from an early-day pioneer family. His grandfather, Henry Fulstone Sr. and grandmother, Elizabeth traveled from Bath, England to New Orleans, U.S.A. in 1855, with sons Henry Jr., Robert, William, Joseph and John. The family joined a wagon train, headed west and stayed in Salt Lake City, Utah, long enough for a baby girl to be born to this family. They paid off debts, and saved money for their journey to California.

These Fulstones stopped in New Empire (now Carson City, Nevada) near what is now the Brewery Arts Building in 1858.

They bought land, raised grass hay and vegetables which they sold in Virginia City, where mining was booming, and people needed food. They even operated a dairy.

Henry Jr. had a son, George, who was born in 1865. George is the grandfather of the Nevada Fulstones. He married Annie Fredericks and this couple had ten children. One of them was Fred Fulstone, born May 4, 1889 in Carson Valley. Fred started school in Genoa, but transferred to Jack's Valley.

George and Annie moved their large family, Harry, Ed, Arthur, Frank, Joseph, Marguerite, Juanita, Clara and Fred, to Wellington, Nevada in 1903. George had purchased the 11,060 acre John Rogers Ranch. Only fifteen to twenty families lived in this expansive land in 1903. George's wife, Annie, worked as a mid-wife in the Smith Valley and Mason Valley areas. Milking the family's cows was one of her farm chores. The cream and butter were sold to the creamery in Minden to help with family expenses. *Mason Valley News,* "Reflections"

The Fulstones bought two more ranches, the Simpson and the Saroni over the next twenty-three years. Fred and three of his brothers helped their father and mother work the land. Crops of every kind grew here – alfalfa, barley, oats, potatoes, onions, garlic. Fred's size, which was tall and muscular, helped him to do the hard ranch work like moving hay, carrying sheep, shoeing horses, clearing rocks, building fences, and digging ditches.

The West Walker River wound through Wellington and Smith Valley providing water for new crops and animals. Both soil and water were good. Fred stayed in Smith Valley and eventually took ownership of a ranch. He had cattle, a large band of sheep, and raised mostly hay and grain for their feed.

Some men are ranchers because they have to be, but Fred Fulstone was a rancher because he loved the land. It responded to his care and success came gradually as the seasons.

Fred was a director of the Walker River Irrigation District. This district built the Topaz Dam, which stored water from the West Walker River, in 1920, and the Bridgeport Dam in 1922, to store water from the East Walker River. He was a member of the Cattle and Woolgrowers Associations, the Farm Bureau and Rotary Club.

Fred Fulstone has been one of the leading ranchers and farmers in this area for many years. He and Dr. Mary have always been among the most prominent and respected citizens of the Smith Valley area. *Nevada – the Silver State.*

CHAPTER THREE

MARY, FRED, AND FAMILY

Mary Hill and Fred Fulstone married on July 16, 1919 in Reno.

Mary chose her husband wisely. He did not feel threatened by his wife's education or career choice. Fred Fulstone was years ahead of his time in this philosophy.

Mary returned to complete her internal medicine residency at San Francisco County Hospital. Fred stayed in Smith Valley, worked the land, raised sheep, and waited for Mary.

In 1920, Mary Hill Fulstone finished her medical residency, then took the Hippocratic Oath:

> "...I do solemnly swear by that which I hold most sacred that, according to my ability and judgment, I will fulfill this oath and this covenant:
>
> That I will be loyal to the medical profession and just and generous to its members and that I will lead my life and practice my art so as to inspire honor and respect from my fellow physicians, my patients, my family and my students so long as I practice.
>
> That I will consider those who taught me this art as dear as my parents and that I will impart my medical knowledge and skills without reservation to those succeeding generations of students who desire to learn and who adhere to the spirit and laws which govern the profession of medicine and to no others.

That I will in deep conscience and forever practice the profession of medicine in full awareness of my limitations of mind
and body so that I will follow that method of treatment which, according to my ability and judgment, I consider best for the benefit
of my patients.

That I will abjure any medicine or operation or counsel
which is injurious or deleterious to my patients or their families.

That I will not, for any reason, refuse my highest abilities
to those who seek my professional skills.

That whatsoever I shall see or hear in regard to the life of
my patients I will keep inviolably in confidence even beyond the
patient's death.

That while I fulfill this oath and do not violate it, may I
enjoy life and art, respected by all persons at all times, but if I
transgress and violate this oath in any measure, may the reverse be
my lot."

Mary Fulstone, M.D., returned to beautiful Smith Valley, began her life with Fred and started her medical practice. She kept regular office hours in their home on the ranch which had been moved
earlier from several miles away to the Fulstone ranch. This large,
eight room house had to be modified later for their big family and for
the privacy of patients.

Months later, Mary gave birth to Fred M. Jr. at the Smith
Valley ranch with Grannie Fulstone's gentle help; Mary's second son,
David Hill waited to be delivered by Dr. Elizabeth Keyes at Children's
Hospital in San Francisco; her third son, Richard Nelson, followed
this pattern; as did the twins, Eleanor and Jeanne, just 19 months af-
ter Richard. Soon they filled the chairs around the large family table.

Now, Mary Hill Fulstone, M.D. kept office hours, made
house calls and was mother of five frisky children.

Once again Fred Fulstone proved that Dr. Mary chose her
husband wisely. He was constantly involved with raising their children. Being a rancher, he usually worked nearby. His time was some-
what flexible. While Daddy Fred irrigated, the children could play
and look for gopher holes to fill. While herding cattle, the children

could ride along on their horses. Of course, everyone could help clean the barn and do other daily chores.

In her oral history, Mary recounted a story that was a family favorite from this period.

The wool buyers came to the front door and asked if Fred was here and Dr. Mary said,

> "Yes, he's around back hanging out laundry." He was, he was putting out the diapers for her. We all got such a kick, because this wool buyer didn't know she was a doctor. He just thought here's that woman sitting there entertaining all those ladies and her poor ol' husband that works on the ranch is out doing the laundry. He was horrified that poor Fred had to put out the laundry, not knowing that Dr. Mary was working too. *Mary Hill Fulstone, M.D. – Oral History.*

Fred Fulstone did not feel belittled when he helped with "women's work." His work ethic and kind ways led Fred to help his family whenever and however he could.

Inside the ranch house framed photographs of the Fulstone children climb the staircase wall – the boys, the girls, all of them together. These children grew up happily as ranch children, tagging along with both Fred and Mary as little ones, but helping out when they were old enough. Sometimes a Paiute or Washo Indian housekeeper or Aunt Jenny Nesmith watched the tiny ones when Fred and Mary were gone. But, until her death in 1933, Grandma Hill cared for the Fulstone "five" most often. Even when Dr. Mary had office hours there was time for her to spend with the children and watch them closely. If she made a house call, the children sometimes rode along in the old pickup. When Mama Mary took too long the children honked the horn to remind her to hurry.

CHAPTER FOUR

DR. MARY: SMITH VALLEY PATIENTS
BUREAU OF INDIAN AFFAIRS CONTRACT

The Paiute Indians who worked on the Fulstone ranch were among Dr. Mary's first patients. They had minor cuts to be cleaned and bandaged. They came with their more serious injuries and illnesses as they learned to trust her. Dr. Mary had a special fondness for these people.

Harriet Arentz became Dr. Mary's closest friend in the valley. She and her children became her patients as well. Two things resulted from this friendship. Other people in the valley became patients because Harriet Arentz came from an influential family. Her husband, Sam Arentz, represented Nevada in the United States Congress. And the Arentz children began calling her "Dr. Mary," instead of "Dr. Fulstone." The Smith Valley people picked up on this and eventually people from all around Nevada called her "Dr. Mary."

Smith Valley had no other doctors, so people who needed help quickly, like those injured in accidents, were glad to have Dr. Mary. Discrimination against a woman doctor rarely raised its ugly head in emergencies.

In the early days of her practice, Dr. Mary was summoned to help a man who had been badly hurt in a horse and wagon turn-over.

She wanted to send him to Reno, but he said, "Oh, no, you're a doctor now and you're supposed to do these things. And you just go ahead and do it." With help from neighbors, she set his broken knee, ankle and dislocated shoulder. He mended nicely and lived for many years with only a little limp. (*Mary Hill Fulstone, M.D., Oral History Program,* University of Nevada, Reno.)

Her size defied the endurance and strength she showed in her life's work. She was just over 5 feet tall and had a small frame. Being petite might have become a problem when she needed super power like trying to pull a dislocated shoulder back into place. However, Dr. Mary was a superb problem solver. In this situation, her solution was to design a leverage system, then find Fred who was a strong and willing helper. She explained, he pulled, and the bone slipped into place. This patient was on the way to recovery.

Just when it seemed as if Dr. Mary had more to do than any one person could handle, something more summoned her. The Indian Agency needed her to serve as the doctor to give medical care to the area's Paiute Indians. She honored the request. Dr. Mary cared for the Paiute Indians. Now she traveled from Smith Valley to Bridgeport, Coleville and Sweetwater at least twice a month and sometimes for emergency calls. This contract with the Indian Agency paid Dr. Mary $90 a month.

The ranchers and their families who settled in Smith Valley learned quickly about the Paiute Indians whose people had lived in the area for thousands of years. They learned these Paiutes lived the primitive lifestyle of their ancestors who roamed to harvest plants and hunt animals until recently when they were interrupted by the new people. The intruders disrupted the environment and made finding food impossible. In the late 1800s the Paiutes were required to live on a reservation, which compounded change in their traditional way of living. Dr. Mary became acquainted with the Paiute men who worked for Fred on the ranch. Their culture was interesting and

Dr. Mary was grateful when they came to her home-office on the ranch for minor medical care. She saw the Paiutes as people with varied needs, like others. Dr. Mary's personality combined with her medical training guided her to be tolerant. This was a beautiful trait in Dr. Mary, and it allowed her more time and energy to be wife, mother, doctor, friend. Also, when one is less judgmental it allows for the development of a sense of humor, for finding fun in life. Dr. Mary always wore a smile and enjoyed laughing; proof that she had left negative thinking behind her.

In her *Oral History,* Dr. Mary explains that she felt no fear of the Paiute People. At first she did worry that a family might get mad at her if she could not help the people.

For example, early in her practice a call came asking Dr. Mary to come to Bridgeport to see Silas B. Smith, a well-known Paiute man. She followed road directions, then walked to the top of a hill with an Indian boy sent to guide her. The Silas B. Smith home was a teepee with a two foot opening for a door. She went through and found a clean, nice living room and a pit with a fire burning. At the other end was a bed with the patient. An oil lamp burned nearby, and his wife sat beside him with her hand on his.

Mrs. Silas B. Smith thanked Dr. Mary for coming. Dr. Mary said she would do her best to help. The patient was very thin and emaciated and he had a terrible pain in his stomach. She examined him, and could feel this mass in his stomach, which was evidently a far-gone cancer. Mrs. Silas B. Smith had him so clean and nice, and had so much hope on her face.

Dr. Mary could give them no hope for recovery, but could leave them some medicine to help his pain. She left them morphine tablets, and kept the memory of this scene always. Peace.

During Dr. Mary's long, long practice, she drove many miles almost every day. She offered Paiute people who were walking a ride. She did this regularly, without fear. They needed a ride, and she was passing that way. From her point of view, it was a simple act of kindness accepted with gratitude. No fear.

Another Paiute story told by Dr. Mary was about a man who believed the house where a relative died should be burned in the traditional way. He burned the house where his wife died so her spirit would not return. Eventually he was sent to prison for this deed.

Dr. Mary wrote letters to convince the authorities he should be released. It was a great victory when he was allowed freedom to return to Smith Valley. Dr. Mary believed in fairness!

Without the help of a few Paiute men, Fred would not have been able to take care of all the needs of ranching. And, without the help of a few Paiute women, through the years, Dr. Mary would not have been able to take care of her medical practice. These Paiute women were trusted, and took good care of the five Fulstone babies and young children.

Dr. Mary needed to be certain there would be an adult presence in her home when she was suddenly called away for an emergency. Many times the emergency was for Dr. Mary to home deliver a baby. The deliveries took long hours, because Dr. Mary arrived at the beginning of labor and stayed until the mother and new baby were stable. The Paiute housekeeper/baby-sitter gave Dr. Mary peace of mind. The children would be fed, clothed, and watched carefully. They would be safe until their mother could return.

When she had time, the Paiute housekeeper might bring her willow threads out and weave them into a basket. Her baskets were to be used in traditional ways like a burden basket to gather pinecones, seed trays and water-tight jugs. Paiute women wove beautiful baskets, and occasionally one was given to the Fulstone family – a treasure shared.

The Paiute people are wonderful storytellers. They have hundreds and hundreds of legends and tales passed down through time.

The Fulstone children might have asked the Paiute housekeeper to tell a story at rest time. One of the favorite stories was about the sea serpents in Walker Lake, which was about thirty-five miles down river from the Fulstone ranch in Smith Valley. It is said that older Paiute people told about seeing two horrible sea serpents living in the lake. Children were warned not to make fun of them because they were very mean.

One day a Paiute said he saw a monster on the bank of Walker Lake. He shot arrows at the animal, but they bounced off him. Then he heated his arrows, and these went into the monster. The story says he returned to this place a year later and found only big bones like ribs scattered on the bank.

From time to time people told of seeing the sea serpents – ugly, over fifty feet long, monsters who smelled terrible. Many Paiute people believed there were sea serpents in Walker Lake. They did not go far into the water. *Walker River Paiutes*

Some people did not believe in the sea serpent story. The editor of the *Lyon County Times* said what people thought was a serpent was more likely a long line of swan or other water fowl which swim on the surface of Walker Lake.

No one has seen or heard about the sea serpents for many years. What has happened to the monsters in Walker Lake? Do they only come out at night? Or, is the last serpent dead? Or something else?

In part because of her service to Native Americans, the U.S. Congress honored her with a resolution on April 8, 1976. It sits on the dining room sideboard. Dr. Mary's many talents and gifts of time and service, including her medical practice for the Paiute Indians, are mentioned in the Resolution. Dr. Mary's family framed this tribute for all guests of the Smith Valley Bed and Breakfast to see – to know Dr. Mary better.

Dr. Mary's medical practice centered around pregnancy, birth, infancy, and childhood. Her medical books still line the shelves of the dining room, and they are inspiring to the touch. Her office is as it was the last time Dr. Mary stepped into it. Overwhelming admiration fills those who see her work place. For over sixty years, people in the area brought their children to her for well-baby checkups, immunization shots, stitches, diagnosis, and treatment of contagious diseases and advice.

Many times, people needed advice most of all. She always listened quietly. She learned while she listened. She learned about people's loves, hates, fears and pain. These clues helped Dr. Mary to suggest ways of solving the problems. She was more than their doctor, she was their valued friend.

Diagnosing difficult symptoms in patients might have been easier as time passed, because many families remained in the valley, and this allowed Dr. Mary to add previous generations' case histories to the current ones. Many times heredity could add all-important information to a complicated diagnosis.

Most of the 4,000 or more babies Dr. Mary delivered were born at home. When summoned she would take her sterile instruments and drive to the home. Fred usually drove her in bad weather - like snow, rain, mud, high winds.

Dr. Mary checked the mother-to-be and talked with her during labor to calm her and quiet her fears. One of her early-day mothers said that Dr. Mary's touch had a healing quality. She checked the linens, baked them and the basins in the oven, if they needed to be sanitized.

No one had hospital beds, so Dr. Mary raised the bed with blocks of wood. Then she put a board under the mattress so the patient could lie across the bed to deliver her baby.

In these early days, there was no electricity, and there were no telephones to help with communication. When labor began Dr. Mary included the father as a "helper." He gave tiny whiffs of chloroform to ease his wife's pain and held the light close for Dr. Mary to see.

Sometimes the father got too much chloroform and put himself to sleep. And sometimes the light disappeared suddenly when the delivery was too much for him. But, whatever happened, Dr. Mary always showed the baby to the proud father herself – a ritual she continued to the last.

Among the hundreds of Dr. Mary "baby stories" there is one which is very telling – The little boy was happy with his new sister, and happy with Dr. Mary, too, because he thought she unselfishly gave them the baby girl from her bag, even though she wanted a girl herself. This story tells of appreciation, sweetness and innocence.

Through the years many wonderful women helped Dr. Mary with baby deliveries. Some of them, like Mrs. Tilley, had a room in their home, clean and ready for a baby's birth and mother's recovery. Others, like Mary Gage, traveled with Dr. Mary to assist during home deliveries. Mrs. Gage also cooked wonderful meals for the new mother and her family.

In an emergency delivery a neighbor might be pulled in to help. One time the twins had to come in from play to be helpers. But the "house calls" gave Dr. Mary the time to get to know her patients and their families; and she claimed them all as friends.

Naturally, Dr. Mary knew from her quality medical training about the dangers of germs. She was diligent in destroying these unseen enemies. Before the 1950s penicillin was nonexistent so it was imperative to sanitize everything that might contaminate the new mother or her baby. Dr. Mary sanitized her own instruments religiously, and she acted as overseer of sanitation in the home. Infections did not erupt here.

Dr. Mary drove from family to family delivering babies safely, and keeping new mothers healthy. Since people had more children at the beginning of her practice, and since Dr. Mary worked throughout the valley, her delivery record was phenomenal. She cared about and followed up on all of her babies, which became known as

"Dr. Mary babies."

Her own health and stamina were remarkable. The ability to organize her medical practice, family life, school boards and more helped her cope with the multitudes of demands on her. Her hair style now was short and curly. It told about her snappy lifestyle which left no time for fancy hairdos.

A sliding-scale helped Dr. Mary decide what fee to charge her patients. In the 1920s and 1930s, she charged $35.00 for a baby delivery, if the people had money. If they had no money, Dr. Mary did not send a bill. During the Depression years, some of Dr. Mary's medical services paid the family grocery store bill. It could be called a barter system. Her fee for one very sick family for a years care was $15.00, because they had so little money.

People in the valley and in Yerington, knew about her generosity. When they could find a way they let her know of their appreciation. Naming the addition of the Lyon County Medical Center the "Dr. Mary Wing" expressed the gratitude and respect felt within the communities.

Social Life

Dr. Mary's hard work and generous nature resulted in people describing her as philanthropic, one who generously promotes human welfare. It is a perfect description of Dr. Mary. The young Mary Hill always kept a demanding schedule. She made time for Loyalty Club at Carson High school, because she liked spending time with friends, and she liked helping with the service projects. At U.C. Berkeley she made time to belong to a sorority, Delta Zeta, even though she studied long and hard.

Practicing medicine and raising children left little free time. But, Dr. Mary continued her pattern by joining Soroptomists who stand for "sincerity of friendship, dignity of service, integrity of profession and love of country." She made new friends, helped with the community projects, served as an officer and was an inspirational speaker throughout northern Nevada.

A longtime Soroptomist from Lovelock, Nevada, said they admired and respected Dr. Mary. And when they scheduled her to be the speaker, members looked forward to hearing meaningful ideas. She said, "Dr. Mary is a true Nevada pioneer."

Dr. Mary found time and energy to belong to the American Association of University Women of Yerington, Delta Kappa Gamma, Beta Sigma Phi and the Eastern Star. Both Fred and Dr. Mary were Episcopalian.

Those who worked with Dr. Mary and her family were well aware of her love for socializing. She was either hostess or guest for an endless number of get-togethers, small and large: like the ladies coming to Dr. Mary's home to make decorations at Christmas time; like the on-going bridge games, parties the nurses put together, the home parties given by Reno doctors, the Farm Bureau dinners, and hospital dedication, holiday parties, school board ceremonies, the L.P.N.'s capping ceremonies, and graduation parties.

Some of the parties were casual but others were quite formal. For example, Dr. Mary was hostess to the State Board of Education for a dinner at the top of the ski resort at Heavenly Valley, Lake Tahoe – elegant!

The question remains though, why did Dr. Mary add these social burdens to her already long list of responsibilities. Without using a psychology text, one guess might be that interacting with friends and family in a positive manner helped her to release tensions tucked away as she worked her way through days of seeing sick or dying patients, doing wonderful but stressful home baby deliveries, and diagnosing, scheduling, and assisting in surgeries. Hard work!

Some people eat or exercise to relieve tensions. Dr. Mary socialized. For example, in her *Oral History* she explained some of the benefits of attending one party.

The hospital Christmas party had become an annual event. It was a dinner and the hospital employees, doctors, nurses, administrator and trustees all attended.

According to Dr. Mary this nice get-together allowed time to talk to people working at the hospital as well as members of the board. It was where she got ideas, and got the feel of how happy the employees were or were not. *Oral History*

Some of her frustrations and stress were relieved at this party.

In 1952 Dr. Mary was sixty years old. She was busily promoting and organizing support for a new hospital in Yerington. She kept office hours in Smith Valley, where her workload almost doubled with the Anaconda mine opening in Yerington. No matter, now she happily helped organize the double wedding and reception for about 200 guests for her twin daughters, Eleanor and Jeanne.

The girls chose to have a large, formal wedding at the Fulstone ranch. They chose beautiful, long gowns, flowers, ribbons and music.

It was a beautiful ceremony July 1, 1952. The brides were dazzling! The wedding was glorious! Guests left with thoughts of wedding bliss. Dr. Mary could fill her pockets with love shared that day.

Will Dr. Mary "do" an anniversary party? The question fluttered around the valley. The answer, of course, was "Yes." Photographs of Dr. Mary and Fred's 50th anniversary show a special celebration. Electricity seemed to shoot through the air between the Fulstone family and their friends – good vibes.

The ranch house stood firm in the background. It was like a frame for the party-goers and the tall, tiered cake. Some guests may have become tired, but Dr. Mary was always rejuvenated with the sharing of happy emotions and events. After the anniversary party, Fred and Dr. Mary must have walked up the ranch house stairs, smiling at the boys, the girls, all of them together, framed on the wall, and turning toward the big, quiet bedroom.

One of the best and largest get-togethers was the reunion in 1980 of Fred's relatives, now Dr. Mary's family too after sixty-one years of marriage. A photograph was taken in honor of the day. Dr. Mary and Fred sit in the center of family members. They are absolutely beaming. Everyone is squeezed back against the fine old house, decorating it along with the country curtains hanging in the windows above them.

About 100 descendants of George and Elizabeth Fulstone had gathered at Dr. Mary and Fred's ranch - a family reunion. Another 50 Fulstones were here to celebrate. All of this group was of the families of Fred, Harry Jr., Frank, Edward, Arthur, Marguerite, Juanita, Clara and Elaine Fulstone. Clara's daughter, Norma Jeanne, had sent invitations and organized a wonderful potluck meal.

Visiting at this party ranged from "familiar" talk to getting "reacquainted". Words spouted like water fountains all day.

Relatives remembered the old, explained the new, and surmising from the photograph were happy for the now.

"A leisure activity is anything an individual chooses to do," says Developmental Psychology Today. Leisure according to Webster's dictionary is time free from work or duties. Socializing equated to leisure and pleasure to Dr. Mary.

Throughout her life, she expressed love of people in social situations. Surprisingly, she benefited emotionally from many of the events. However, there was never any doubt Dr. Mary cared about her patients most. She always went to them immediately when summoned even if it meant missing a wedding, or hospital dedication, or wedding shower at her house.

Even though Dr. Mary was 88 years old and Fred was 91, they were delighted to have this family reunion at the Smith Valley Ranch, their home. One photograph of the day captured facial expressions that expressed the extraordinary feelings of family togetherness and pride.

Host Fred and hostess Dr. Mary, made family welcome, carried out their responsibilities, no doubt relived and relished the day, reflected on family, and finally must have rested on the soft chintz living room sofa.

CHAPTER FIVE

DR. MARY:
YERINGTON PATIENTS HOSPITAL ROUNDS

Dr. Mary's medical practice expanded to Yerington, Nevada, two and then three days a week in the late 1940s, when the five Fulstone children were older, and when Yerington had only one exhausted physician, Dr. Marvin Beams. Dr. Mary was sometimes teased about driving this 25 miles so fast. She was a busy lady and could not lose a minute on the road.

Major support for medical projects in Yerington came from local newspapers as well as from newspapers around the state. The *Mason Valley News* staff, Walter Cox and Bob Sanford, even served on the selection board for Licensed Practical Nurses. Dr. Mary openly appreciated the media's "kindness" to medicine.

In 1952 Yerington had only a small building which served as shelter for eight to ten elderly men who could not live alone, and as an emergency room for surgery. People in this rural community went to Reno, which was eighty miles away, for hospital care and planned surgery.

Dr. Mary was certain the time was right for Yerington to build a hospital. She reasoned that the cumulative population of the town and two valleys, plus the new Anaconda Mine people warranted local hospital care and this would be economically feasible. She advocated for a new Lyon County Health Facility for several years. Finally when Albert (Archie) Millar, Manager of Anaconda Mines, was convinced this project was needed, he promised that his people (about 500 employees) would use the facility. This promise meant economic success for a new health facility without there being a huge burden on the communities.

This did not look like a "boom and bust" operation. It was not. From 1951 to 1977 the Anaconda Mine operated at peek level, and until 1999, mining companies were leasing the processing area to remine the tailings using new technologies.

For a twenty-six year period, Anaconda's Annual payroll was $3,500,000. Lewis Nordyke "Mining with Anaconda" in *The Explosives Engineer.*

With Anaconda's backing, the people in Lyon County passed a bond for a hospital - $150,000 on April 14, 1953. A grant from Hill-Burton, a Federal Fund, covered the balance.

On March 24, 1954, the Lyon Health Center was completed. Dr. Maclean, from Carson City, performed three major and four minor surgeries on the second day the new hospital was open. These surgery patients and their families were spared the multiple trips to and from Reno.

Rules and regulations in the charter were followed; charts were kept, and records were organized. National accreditation was awarded to this rural hospital. *Oral History and Lyon County Clerk's Office.*

Dreams came true! Her people would now have better, safer care at home in the local hospital.

At first the people of Yerington and farmers and ranchers from Mason Valley and Smith Valley questioned the idea that Anaconda Mine people would be in the area long enough to help pay for a hospital bond. But, in less than two years, 1951 and 1952,

Anaconda had developed plant facilities, the mine site, built a town and begun open-pit copper mining.

The company townsite was appropriately named Weed Heights, in honor of Clyde E. Weed, Chairman of the Board of Directors of the Anaconda Company. It consisted of about 250 houses, a post office, a swimming pool, basketball court, tennis courts, children's playground, picnic area, golf course, and softball field. Weed Heights even had its own Zip Code. "Anaconda Copper Mine," Records Department, Yerington, Nevada.

Then Dr. Mary helped to organize a courtesy staff of physicians from Reno and Carson City, Nevada, to rotate out to Yerington for surgery, orthopedics, obstetrics for cesareans, internal medicine, pediatrics, neurology and other specialties.

To get the rotating physicians out for a required annual staff meeting, Dr. Mary organized a family pheasant hunt and picnic at the Fulstone ranch. Fred Sr. fired his shotgun to start the hunt at precisely 8:00 a.m. The families had fun and the doctor's staff meeting took the shortest time possible. This tradition continued through Dr. Mary's life and was considered to be one of the finest social events in the valley. (Appendix II).

When Medicare regulations took much of the control of a patient out of the doctor's hands, Dr. Mary wondered if this program really cared whether people got well. Medicare dictated what tests a patient should have, what medicine, and how long a hospital stay should be without ever seeing the patient.

Dr. Mary found time and energy to serve as Chief of Staff for Lyon Health Center and also as Lyon County Physician. So now she handled administrative matters as well as medical. Her Yerington office was in the home of Elizabeth Post who served as Dr. Mary's office nurse for many years. They were fast friends.

Lion County Hospital

State Board of Health

Legislature passed legislation enabling the State to take advantage of Federal grants for assisting with hospital construction as provided under Public Law 725 of the 79th Congress.

State of Nevada

Biennial Report of the

State Board of Health

July 1, 1952 to June 30, 1954

Hospital Bond Issue

The estimated cost of the Lyon County Hospital was $350,000, so the County would pay $117,000 as its share. The government (under Hill-Burton) would pay $234,000 as its share.

Lyon County Commissioners asked for $150,000 in bonds.

Legal notices were prepared by the District Attorney for the election and bond issue. Taxpayers would pay an additional fourteen cents on each $100 valuation yearly, to provide the County's share. *Mason Valley News,* Jan. 9, 1953

Funding for Lyon County Hospital

Lyon County residents have the opportunity to get assistance from the Federal Government in the amount of two-thirds of the cost of the total hospital project. This is a grant made possible under the Hill-Burton Act for emergency aid to counties in great need of hospitalization. *Mason Valley News,* March 20, 1953.

Election

An election was set for Saturday, April 4, 1953, for the purpose of authorizing a $150,000 bond issue for a new Lyon County Hospital. *Mason Valley News,* February 20, 1953 and March 20, 1953.

Bond Issue Passed

Registered voters from Mason Valley, Smith Valley, Weed Heights, Dayton, Silver City, and all of Lyon County voted: 821 votes of approval to 40 votes against for the hospital bond issue.

Mason Valley News, April 10, 1953

Hospital Board

Louis Isola, A.E. MacKenzie, Claude Rife, Frank Godwin and Norman Brown were elected to the new Hospital Board of Trustees. Norman Brown was named chairman of the Board. Louis Isola will serve as vice-president. These men were nominated for the hospital service by the Board of County Commissioners.

The board members were to have complete charge of the operation of the new hospital, and were to decide on the type of building to be constructed and the equipment to be installed. The State Health Department was to serve as consultant.

Mason Valley News, April 10, 1953

CHAPTER SIX

SMITH VALLEY SCHOOL BOARD
AND STATE BOARD OF EDUCATION

Her ongoing respect for education resulted in Mary's decision to serve on the local School Board for twenty-four years. During one term on the Smith Valley School Board, Dr. Mary served as president and had the honor or handing out the high school diplomas. She realized that she had delivered all of the graduating students. Dr. Mary had a phrase for that kind of happening – "heart squeezing"; and so it was for many.

When the five frisky Fulstone children put their heads together, they usually had hilarious ideas and made good plans. Since the school board meeting was at their house, they decided to get out of bed and creep down the stairs to hear all of the important Smith Valley School District secrets. But they barely got arranged on the stairs when Dr. Mary, who rarely missed anything, caught the night creepers and shooed them off to bed. It might have been fun to eavesdrop a bit longer, but no matter, this adventure was exciting; and there would be a next time.

Serving a small, rural area with a limited budget, the Smith Valley Consolidated School District decided to rely on its citizens to supplement their students' experiences and knowledge. For example, a rancher might be asked to teach a unit on agricultural economics; or a retired airline pilot might be asked to lecture on air transportation. It was a good way to learn. This practice ended abruptly, however, when a bill was passed which required all instructors to be college graduates with some education credits. Now the school board members wondered how they could fill the gap left by the community instructors. Dr. Mary decided she would help by giving up her seat on the board in favor of younger members with new ideas.

Just months later, Richard Fulstone, son of Dr. Mary, joined the Smith Valley School Board and served for the next sixteen years.

This generation might have creative ideas to solve difficult school district problems. Undoubtedly, Dr. Mary envisioned help for education from these new board members.

In 1957, the Nevada State Board of Education lost a board member. Dr. Mary's name was proposed to fill the seat, and she was asked to finish this term. Dr. Mary agreed to serve. She traveled to Carson City, Reno, or Las Vegas, for board meetings about once a month. They usually began at 10:00 a.m. and finished by 4:00 p.m. Even though time consuming, Dr. Mary recognized the importance of a diversified board. She could be resolute without being volatile. She could be persuasive without being dictatorial. She could listen. Her goal was for the State of Nevada to provide educational opportunities for every student.

She melded the State Board meetings and decision making duties into her medical practice and family responsibilities; and influenced statewide direction of public education in Nevada. She approved of strict rules in the schools and disapproved of programs that experimented with curriculum.

Dr. Mary liked the career training curriculum because it got away from the idea that every child should go to college. It provided vocational classes as an alternative.

The Board followed a certain amount of ceremony. For example, "The Honorable Cameron Batjer, Justice, Nevada Supreme Court, with due ceremony, administered the oaths of office to the seven elected members of the Nevada State Board of Education." From January 7, 1971, *State Board Minutes.*

Dr. Mary was beginning her third term on the State Board of Education at this time. She was especially proud because Judge Batjer of the Nevada Supreme Court, grew up in Smith Valley.

At the June 4, 1970 Board meeting in Reno, Nevada, "Consideration was given to the request of the Churchill County School District for waiver of transportation regulations to allow busing of secondary school pupils and one elementary school pupil, from Dixie Valley to Fallon. Discussion of the problem was held as well as consideration of alternative proposals for solving the elementary pupil's transportation problem. Such proposals included 'in-lieu-of' payments by the District to the parents of the child; transportation to Fallon by parents, if feasible; excusing the child from attending school in Fallon with a home-study course instituted; reopening the Dixie Valley school if it should develop that five or six elementary students would be living in the area."

"Upon motion by Dr. Fulstone, seconded by Mr. Vacchina and unanimously carried, the State Board of Education granted the request of the Churchill County School District for a waiver of regulations in transporting secondary school pupils (grades 7-12) for the 1970-71 school year, from Dixie Valley to Fallon and return, and denied the request for waiver of regulations in transporting the elementary school pupil. The District is to be advised of the suggested alternate proposals for education of the elementary school pupil."

Dr. Mary took the lead in settling this weighty problem. She was not faint hearted. She helped find solutions.

Dr. Mary's third term expired December 31, 1976, and she chose not to seek reelection. She was eighty-four years old and had rarely missed a meeting in 19 years on the State Board. Even now Dr. Mary seemed younger than her years. Her enthusiasm for life joined her in each brisk step. It wiped away the years. Those who depended on her for medical help and friendship had come to expect that she would live forever.

CHAPTER SEVEN

MARY'S PRAISE FOR FRED AND FAMILY

Continuing up the ranch house stairs, photographs of the Fulstones smile cordially. The picture of Eleanor and Jeanne was taken when they won the Toni Twins Contest of 1950s home permanent fame. Dr. Mary felt great pride in the girls for this honor.

But, can the marriage of a rural Nevada rancher to a family-practice doctor last? This question fluttered about the valley periodically. The answer sits in a frame on the piano in the comfortable living room. Dr. Mary and Fred Fulstone are shown celebrating the 50th year of their marriage in 1969. Family and friends are shown in another photograph joining in the anniversary celebration. The answer, of course, is a jubilant, "Yes!"

As if this 50th wedding celebration were not enough, another spectacular event was in progress – the moon landing. Neal Armstrong and Buzz Aldren, our United States Astronauts, had been hurtling through space toward the moon and were, at this very minute, preparing for the unimaginable landing and walk on the moon.

Will their spaceship get them to the moon? Will they land safely? Will they accomplish the experiments? Will they get back to earth alive?

According to one of Dr. Mary and Fred's guests, Fred Sr. waved his hands and said, "They're helping us celebrate."

Dr. Mary told Mary Ellen Glass, the University of Nevada, Reno oral historian, "I just sometimes think how lucky I am that I had such a good husband. I don't suppose I'd ever been able to (have a medical practice) like I did if I had a different type of husband."

The friendliness of Dr. Mary's home reaches into the soul. Immediately, a smile comes to visitors' faces. Then a deep desire emerges; a need to know more about Mary Hill Fulstone, the Nevada pioneer.

For example: To say Dr. Mary was thrilled when word reached her that the University in Reno might get a medical school would be an understatement.

Dr. Mary was an eager and early supporter of the University Medical School. Her support was crucial in getting State Assemblyman Joe Dini, D, Yerington, and others behind the medical school project.

The University of Nevada Medical School opened its door to students in 1969. Classroom studies began and a rotation schedule was required for each student. Robin Titus did a rotation with Dr. Mary, who might be called her mentor. When Robin finished medical school and residency she began a medical practice in Smith Valley. Dr. Titus's practice is appreciated in this rural area, and continues to flourish in 2001. Thanks, in part, to Dr. Mary!

For example, some people wondered about Dr. Mary's values. When asked, Dr. Mary denied being a feminist, only ambitious. In a 1973 *Nevada State Journal* article she said, "You get your rights, your needs met, through your own efforts." But, Dr. Mary, wouldn't ambition lead you to live in a big city with well-equipped hospitals, where prestigious doctors perform surgical miracles? Wouldn't it lead you to accept the Mayo Clinic appointment offered to you during your medical residency?

Mary's husband-to-be, Fred Fulstone, owned land in Smith Valley with its soft green grasses and rich brown soil. Was not this enough reason to prepare for a family practice in rural Nevada?
It was for Mary Hill.

At the top of the stairs, and to the right, Dr. Mary and Fred had a large bedroom. The old oak rocking chair by the window is a reminder of times past – early motherhood and fatherhood. This room, slightly away from the others, held something important - "quiet." It was a refuge for Dr. Mary and Fred.

The other three bedrooms spoke of busy older children - a jewelry box and frilly lamp shade speak of girls. In the other bedrooms footballs, basketballs, boots say, the boys.

Coming downstairs to the huge kitchen, visitors can sit at the round oak table and see some of the ranch out of the window. What a wonderful way for the Fulstones to start each "growing-up" day.

> The calm without brings calm within
> and the closeness of nature
> offers a closeness to the heavens.
> "All is well, all is well."
>
> *Poem by Dixie Westergard*

The Fulstone Five – Fred Jr., David, Richard, Jeanne, and Eleanor, were growing up. Only the twins were at the University of Nevada now. Dr. Mary might have seen this change as a chance to be with friends or play bridge more often which had been a passion since her own college days.

Instead she kept her Smith Valley office hours at 8:00–11:00. She increased her Yerington hospital rounds from two to four days a week from 12:30–2:30, and she increased her Yerington office hours from 2:30–6:00 or later four days a week, seeing about 30 people each afternoon. Emergencies took precedence over routine, and baby deliveries were often a primary emergency. Even board meetings took precedence over a quiet evening or day at the ranch.

Instead of slowing down, Dr. Mary stepped up her working hours. This meant she had even less time for herself.

Long days left Dr. Mary tired, but never weary. It might have been her well-known sense of humor that kept her so lively and ready for laughter. She had hundreds of stories and enjoyed sharing them – often to make a clever point.

From her *Oral History,* comes this remembrance. A lady walked up to the twins as they played in the sand at Lake Tahoe. She said, "Your mother is the doctor, does she practice?"

"Oh no, she knows how," the twins answered. Dr. Mary liked this story. It made her laugh; but then it reminded her that people are curious about a woman doctor in rural Nevada. But, at the same time, her girls accepted their mother's work without question.

Time is a doctor's sacrifice. But in spite of missing parties, and school activities due to emergencies, Dr. Mary considered her family "close-knit," with a happy life. They did things together like helping Fred with the sheep on camp tender's day; when he delivered supplies to the other herders; and singing and playing the piano in the evenings. They did most things together.

Dr. Mary bought a baby grand piano with the first "hard" money she earned from her rural medical practice. She played her piano and everyone in the house sang. Some danced. They could be as loud and late as they wished because no one lived within miles.

One of the twins has Dr. Mary's piano. It sits in her home now, a treasure shared.

Another piano sits in the Smith Valley ranch house. It was a gift from a family member who thought the living room needed a piano to complete its story.

Fred and the extended family continually helped Dr. Mary keep the Fulstones close.

The Fred Fulstone, Sr. house has more to say through the lives lived in it and the examples shown through them:

Live in harmony
helping along the way

Leave your weaknesses
far, far behind

Pursue your dreams
learning all the time.
                Poem by Dixie Westergard

Lake Tahoe means something different to everyone. Those who connect with its beauty – perfection can never get enough of her offerings to be satisfied. Often a passion for a "place" begins early in life, in childhood. It is like a secret being added to periodically by a visit, a story, a picture, or even a fragrance. Good feelings surface.

Sharing the "place" compounds it as a treasure. Dr. Mary began loving Lake Tahoe in childhood. She expanded her special feelings by introducing her own family to the lake. One of Dr. Mary and Fred's twins has been living at the lake for years.

The feeling of the "place" can transcend touch. By concentrating sights, sounds, and smells can be brought up to the conscious level. The value of this trait is limitless.

As life compounds schedules, it can become almost impossible to get to the "place." Usually a solution can be found. For Dr. Mary the answer was to buy a summer cabin near the lake at Marla Bay. Now she and her family could stay over instead of speeding back about fifty-five miles to Smith Valley. Logistics made it easier to visit Lake Tahoe.

The beauty of Lake Tahoe with its blue snow water, white sand beaches; and ring of pine scented mountains offers comfort to the soul. It can provide safety from the worries of the world.

People who knew Dr. Mary talked about her love for Lake Tahoe. She practically ran through life to meet her responsibilities but she managed to visit the lake even in busy times. When she saw it, the message was to "relax, enjoy".

The Lake Tahoe cabin, which was purchased in the 1930s and served as a haven to Dr. Mary, remains in the Fulstone family - a treasure shared.

Renewal
The lake shared its pure water
with me a splash at a time
Then, feeling more friendly
In a little wave
The pine held its long limbs
about me with tenderness
The limbs kept me safe from
the worries of the world
I like the friendliness and
comfort of this place
Lake Tahoe is where
I need to be

Poem by Dixie Westergard

Dr. Mary tells so charmingly about the Fulstone Family's perception of monetary worth in her *Oral History*.

"I always think about Freddie (Fred M. Fulstone, Jr.) when he graduated from high school (laughs). He got a new suit of clothes, and he thought it was just going to break the family to get him a new suit of clothes. I was going to get him a new pair of shoes and he said, "On, no Mother. You can't afford another pair of shoes." But that suit of clothes (laughs) – David (David Hill Fulstone) was married in it, Johnnie Nesmith (Jenny's son) was married in it (laughs). Freddie was married in it a little later, so I don't know how many it served. They all graduated in it. So that's the kind of a life we had, but still we were very happy. And we almost felt we were affluent, you know. Of course, the Depression came in those years."

The three Fulstone boys - Fred, David, Richard - attended the University of Nevada; Richard graduated and they all continued in agriculture in Smith Valley and Yerington. The girls, Jeanne and

Eleanor graduated from the University of Nevada, taught school and eventually settled in Sacramento, California and Lake Tahoe, Zephyr Cove, Nevada respectively.

In 1982 an article entitled "She's Nevada's Favorite Doctor" was written for the *Pacific Southern Airlines Magazine*. It summarized Dr. Mary's medical career by saying, "A mixture of love and know-how is Mary Fulstone's prescription for successfully practicing medicine longer than any other doctor in Nevada – 62 years." Finally the article said that "Fred was still by Dr. Mary's side."

When talking with Mary Ellen Glass, University of Nevada's Oral Historian, Dr. Mary said more about her husband, Fred. "He has really accomplished a great deal in his life. He's been busy and interested and doing things all the time, you know. He's 85 years old now and he goes out and separates cattle and vaccinates and feeds and everything else." *Oral History*.

Fred died at age 95 in 1985, after a short illness. He is buried in the Smith Valley cemetery. His headstone is embellished with a lamb which is a reminder of the importance of ranching in his life.

CHAPTER EIGHT

ADVANCEMENTS IN MEDICAL TECHNOLOGY

According to a member of her family, when Dr. Mary examined a patient she concentrated on the injury, the illness or baby delivery circumstances without discussing the technicalities of medicine. Finishing with the formal part of her visit, she would indulge happily in exchanges about personal and community events, just chat. Dr. Mary assumed sick people were not interested in technology. They were interested in getting well.

Becoming an M.D. was only the beginning of Dr. Mary's gathering of technical medical knowledge. As new developments sprang forth, she grasped them, learned how to use the new medicine or complicated technique, and applied them to her patient's benefit.

Many medical advancements were made after Dr. Mary began practicing medicine in 1920. The following diseases and illnesses were great threats to the health and well-being of people before medical technology devised vaccines, antibiotics, sulfa drugs, gamma globulin, insulin and other remedies.

Diabetes

Symptoms, causes, cures: Loss of weight, fatigue, frequent urination, thirst, muscle cramps, blurred vision, lingering infections or slow healing wounds. Excessive amounts of sugar in the blood and urine. The body does not regulate the level of "sugar" or glucose in the blood. Caused by heredity and lifestyle. Insulin helps to control symptoms.

Diphtheria

Symptoms, causes, cures: Headache, fever and severe sore throat; white covering over tonsils, throat and soft palate. Fever 101 degrees to 103 degrees. There may be difficult swallowing, a croupy cough and bloody discharge from nose. Spread by contact. Vaccine, DPT – Diphtheria, Pertussis (whooping cough), Tetanus.

Epilepsy

Symptoms, causes, cures: Grand mal seizures, loss of consciousness and stiffening of body; a fall to the ground and stiffening of muscles. Petit mal epilepsy has no seizures, but a short loss of consciousness. Caused by heredity, illness or injury in brain. Controlled by medication.

Flu - influenza – Type A, B, Asian Viruses

Symptoms, causes, cures: Headache, fatigue, chills, aches and pains in arms, legs and back. Nose congested. Hard, dry cough. Spread by contact. Antibiotics given for bacterial complications.

Hepatitis

Symptoms, causes, cures: Weakness, fatigue, dark urine, light stools, itching skin and jaundice. A viral infection of liver. Spread by contact. Gamma globulin given.

Infantile paralysis – polio

Symptoms, causes, cures: fever, vomiting and irritability; severe headache, high fever 102 degrees to 103 degrees, and a stiff neck and back. Pain and atrophy in muscles. Paralysis occurs 10 to 15% of cases. Disability and deformity often occur. Spread by contact. Vaccine given.

Polio Treatment - During the 1930s, when polio was striking down people worldwide, George Washington Carver suggested deep muscle massage using peanut oil. An accomplished masseur, Carver treated several polio victims who showed marked improvement. Carver even gave a bottle of peanut oil to President Franklin Roosevelt, himself a polio victim.

Reno Gazette Journal - March 10, 2002

Pernicious anemia

Symptoms, causes, cures: Vitamin B12 is not absorbed; numbness or tingling of hands or feet, staggering walk, loss of control of bowel and bladder function. The blood is deficient in red blood cells, in hemoglobin or in volume. Vitamin B12 given by injection, through food.

Pertussis – Whooping Cough

Symptoms, causes, cures: Dry cough gets more severe at night; third week cough is severe, spasmodic, repetitive (person may lose breath and become blue - vomits); mucus in the bronchi is thick and sticky. Asphyxia does not occur, but pneumonia can result. Spread by contact. Vaccine given - DPT.

NOTE: Whooping cough swept through Smith Valley, and many of the children became sick. All of the Fred and Mary Fulstone children came down with whooping cough.

Medical researchers were working on a vaccine to prevent whooping cough, but it was not ready yet.

Pneumonia

Symptoms, causes, cures: Cough, fever, rapid breathing, pain in chest, production of phlegm which is sometimes blood stained.

Especially dangerous for the young and old. Caused by infection or irritants. Antibiotics given for bacterial infection.

Tetanus

Symptoms, causes, cures: Increasing stiffness of jaw until difficult to open mouth. Later, stiffness of back and abdominal muscles with neck thrown back and back curved in; spasms of muscles are excruciatingly painful. Contracted from bacillus germ in the soil, usually through a wound. Vaccine given - DPT.

Tuberculosis – T.B.

Symptoms, causes, cures: Low grade fever, mild viral infection, and dry cough. If infection spreads through blood stream more severe symptoms occur; T.B. can become chronic. Spread by contact. Caused by a bacteria. Antibiotics given.

Vaccination

Principle: Small dose of killed germs, or weakened live virus is administered to build the body's natural defenses against the disease. Diseases for which we routinely immunize are: diphtheria, Pertussis (whooping cough), tetanus, measles, mumps, rubella, poliomyelitis, smallpox. Newly developed vaccines become available with research. *Better Homes and Gardens, New Family Medical Guide.*

Mary Ellen Glass, Oral Historian, asked for Dr. Mary to comment on the advancements in medical technology during her career. The response was spirited as she talked about her horrible encounter with the 1918 flu epidemic when there was no medicine for flu and massive numbers of deaths occurred. In her talk with Mary Ellen Glass she praised researchers for developing antibiotics. With the use of penicillin and other medicine a flu patient was rarely lost.

Each year dozens of cases of tuberculosis flared up in the valley. Now these people and pneumonia patients could be cured with the use of antibiotics.

Next Dr. Mary talked about diphtheria, whooping cough and tetanus. She explained that whooping cough was especially bad because it spread easily, and could be fatal. Then the DPT vaccination was developed and it irradicated these three diseases. Dr. Mary was an avid advocate of vaccinations. She gave them at schools as well as in her offices in Smith Valley and Yerington.

Another terrible disease was polio - infantile paralysis. After the preventative vaccine was introduced there were no more cases in the valley. Dr. Mary said it was a great relief.

Even though hepatitis could not be cured, through research it was learned that giving gamma globulin to those exposed would keep them well.

Dr. Mary explained that sulfa drugs were developed when researchers noticed at a dyeing factory that sulfa got into the cells and nuclei of material fast. By transferring information, researchers tried putting sulfa into people's blood and cells. This worked. The use of sulfa drugs stopped many diseases!

Dr. Mary delighted in telling about anticoagulants, possibly because the discovery came from a farm. The problem was that after dehorning, the cattle bled, many died. Researches found the cattle were eating clover containing cumadon and danolin. These ingredients kept the dehorned cattle's blood from clotting. Researchers used this information in reverse order. They used cumadon and danolin for heart patients who needed thinner blood.

Since Dr. Mary graduated from medical school, discoveries of insulin for diabetes, B-12 for pernicious anemia, and medicines for epilepsy were made. "Really wonderful things like that!" she said. So many discoveries had been made that it was fascinating for Dr. Mary to continue to study medicine and try to work out a regimen for each patient's needs.

New techniques were developed which made heart surgery possible. Soon after remarkable intensive care units were developed to provide the expertise needed to care for these special patients. Finally, Dr. Mary found it wonderful to see the changes in medicine through the years. She was proud of medical accomplishments and was optimistic about future developments like cancer cures.

Throughout her medical career, Dr. Mary gathered, absorbed, and used new developments in technology. Three generations of patients are testament to her passion for medicine and success in practicing it. Mary Hill Fulstone, M.D. – *Oral History.*

CHAPTER NINE

CONCLUSION

Both Fred and Dr. Mary lived into their 95th year; Fred still ranching and Dr. Mary still practicing medicine.

In her *Oral History,* Dr. Mary explained her passion for rural medicine. She said, "There is something special and fulfilling about being a rural doctor. It's the people who make it so. It's like being part of each family."

According to an article in the *Nevada State Journal,* October 31, 1979, Dr. Mary now eighty-eight years old, was still making house calls. Remarkable! Even more astounding is the fact Dr. Mary delivered her own great granddaughter, Kimber Lee, at this time.

After 60 years of practicing medicine, she happily continued to help those who needed her care. However, now she depended on help with driving. Her eyesight was failing, but she still had meetings to attend and patients to visit.

Dr. Mary's mental and physical stamina kept her going. Her basic love of people helped her to meet their medical needs.

In her 95th year, Dr. Mary suffered a severe stroke. Nevada was losing a saint, a renowned physician who always answered when summoned – day or night, fair weather or foul. She lay in the front bedroom of the ranch house. Members of her family sat with her until the end. Each one, no doubt embracing memories of her compassionate life.

Perhaps one person thought about the 4,000 babies Dr. Mary home delivered; another may have thought about her amazing "courtesy staff" of medical specialists; then some might have thought about Dr. Mary and Fred, the love story underlying all.

Dr. Mary died in the front bedroom of the Fulstone ranch house just two years after Fred, in 1987. She is buried next to him in the Smith Valley cemetery. The symbol for medical doctor embellishes her headstone as a reminder to all who visit of the importance of medicine in her life.

This biography of Mary Hill Fulstone, M.D. is a tribute to her passion for medicine and compassion for people. At the same time, the biography is meant to inspire and encourage people to boldly set goals, struggle, if necessary, to achieve the goals and embrace life.

As you leave her home you know her, and she has touched you, the great Nevada Pioneer, Mary Fulstone, M.D.

EPILOGUE

A tape recording of Dr. Mary speaking to the Cowbelles in the 1980s gave a fine understanding of her persona. Her voice conveys excitement and energy as she tells anecdotes of a woman, rural doctor in the early 1900's. She liked to laugh and she liked to hear others laugh. As she explained each event, the thoughts move from silly to serious – a Dr. Mary trait. Dr. Mary finished her talk by expressing admiration for researchers who brought antibiotics like penicillin, vaccines for immunizations and improved methods of treatment to the field of medicine. She expressed appreciation for these medical advances which helped doctors cure the sick or injured ones in their care. Dr. Mary conveyed this information about the scientific world easily and with relish. Her energy level did not wane as she talked; but occasionally she worried that her listeners might be getting tired. Deciding not yet, after glancing around, Dr. Mary charged ahead.... She told the "cowbelles" that the closest she personally ever got to the livestock business was when a patient paid his bill with a "big ole pig". (Here her voice lilts and the laugh in it is almost palpable). Fred took care of the pig-feeding, watering, sheltering while trying to find a buyer. Months later Fred sold the pig for $360. His bill for feed was $362. The Cowbelles laughed with Dr. Mary as she lamented not coming out too well with that pig.

There was no doubt that Dr. Mary was a very, very intelligent physician - strong of will, but gentle in persuasion. Her sincerity and caring qualities were not shouted. They emerged between and around thoughts, and it is certain that the world is a better place because of her.

AWARDS FOR DR. MARY

Awards help to tell the story of a remarkable woman, a pioneer in rural Nevada:

Mary Fulstone, M.D.

1950 – Nevada Mother of Year

1961 – Woman of the Year – Delta Zeta Sorority

1963 – Nevada Doctor of the Year – Nevada Medical Association

1963 – A.K. Robbins Award / Outstanding Community Service by a Physician

1963 – A plaque at the Lyon Health Center says: "Dedicated to our Dr. Mary Fulstone, whose medical skill and helping hand have protected and guided us through many years; a faithful wife, loving mother, and philanthropist to all mankind."

1964 – University of Nevada Distinguished Nevadan Award

1964 – Gold Rose Emblem by Delta Zeta Sorority – 50 Year Alumni

1970 – U.C.–Berkeley Certificate for Fifty Years Medical Practice

1976 – Congressional Register Tribute – placed by Nevada Senator Paul Laxalt

1976 – Distinguished Service in Medical Practice Silver Plate – engraved, "She is a friend, an inspiration, a colleague who is the highest credit to our profession, a humanitarian in the fullest sense of the word!"

1976 – Devoted Service Award, U.N.R. School of Medicine

1979 – Soroptomist Woman of Achievement Award

1979 – Grand Marshal of Nevada Day Parade (Dr. Mary and Fred)

1981 – Salvation Army's "Others Award" in recognition of her lifetime of service to her fellow man.

1984 – Inducted into the Nevada Women's Fund Hall of Fame

2001 – Nominated for Nevada Women's History Project Roll of Honor

COURTESY STAFF

It's been especially nice, because we've had this help from what we call our "courtesy staff." We started the system in asking the surgeons, the medical people and the orthopedic people, specialists in Reno, to come out for certain days and do surgery. And many came out and operated. We have operations every day and neither Dr. Beams or I are surgeons. Dr. [Kenneth] Maclean was one of our biggest boosters and the biggest helpers because he was about the first one that would come out and do surgery for us and show us how things should be done.

Then Dr. [Donald] Guisto came for years. Finally, I think their practice became so large there that they couldn't hardly spare the days that they came out. Dr. [J. Malcolm] Edmiston has been coming for a number of years, still comes, and Dr. [Edwin W.] Prentice comes. We have Dr. [James R.] Herz, occasionally, who flies out and does orthopedic surgery for us. Dr. [Emanuel] Berger has come out for pediatrics, and Dr. [Adolf] Rosenauer and Dr. [Ernest] Mack for the neurological department when we needed help, were always very accommodating. Then Dr. [John W.] Brophy has been our big supporter for many years. He comes down and does the nose and throat work. He comes once or twice every month. And is always available for consultations. We had a roentgenologist, Dr. [Harry B.] Gilbert, from Reno who has come once every week and does the fluoroscopy work and reads every picture. Every x-ray that's taken in the hospital is read by Dr. Gilbert or his assistant.

Oh, and Dr. [Joseph Park] Tuttle, I should mention him. He was a great help to us in our early days. He has retired now. He was a GU man. And in obstetrics if we had to have a cesarean, why, usually one of the obstetricians will come out and do a cesarean for you. Dr. [Frank V.] Rueckl comes out now. And Dr. [Henry] Stewart has come out in the past. Doctors [Peter] Rowe, [Joseph S.] Phalen, and [David S.] Thompson come out on consultation in internal medicine; and others.

One of the best things about this hospital is that we have this "courtesy staff" that's standing by to help us on all of our problems. They have been a great big support for us. They come out once a year to a staff meeting which is in our staff rules. In order to get them out and to be sure that they'll come to the meetings – a bunch of doctors aren't going to give up a whole night and just come out and have dinner and a meeting – I instituted the pheasant hunting day.

The day that the pheasant hunting is open, all these doctors are invited out to our ranch to hunt pheasants. Then we have dinner for them, and our meeting. They bring their wives and all their children. Some of them have come each year when the children were little and now they're all grown up, like Dr. [William M.] Tappan's sons, for instance. That has worked out very well so that we usually have a very good "courtesy staff" meeting every year. For years when we haven't had pheasants, why, we bought the pheasants and put them on the ranch so that they all get a pheasant. It's been a little trick, I guess, to get them out here; but you can see yourself it would be hard, because it would take pretty near a day, you know, to drive out and have the meeting and drive back. And [it] would have to be a Sunday. All the doctors like it, I think. That's their favorite thing about the hospital." *Oral History, Mary Hill Fulstone, M.D.*

Arlington Hotel, Carson City, Nevada, 1890s. *Nevada State Museum.*

Capitol grounds, with band stand for summer concerts, Carson City, Nevada, 1890s. *Nevada State Museum.*

Mary Hill and her friends took the Steamer Tahoe around Lake Tahoe in about 1910, much the same as this sightseeing tour in front of Tallac Resort. *Roland Westergard Family Collection.*

Fred Fulstone, 1912 (about 23 years old). *Norma Jean Hesse Wallace Collection.*

Championship high school basketball team–
Carson High School. c. 1910. Coach
W. J. Hunting and the girls (Mary Hill
far right). *Fulstone Family Collection.*

Mary Ruth Hill, yearbook photograph, University of
California Berkeley, 1914. *Special Collections University
of California Berkeley (Call # 308s B6 1915:459).*

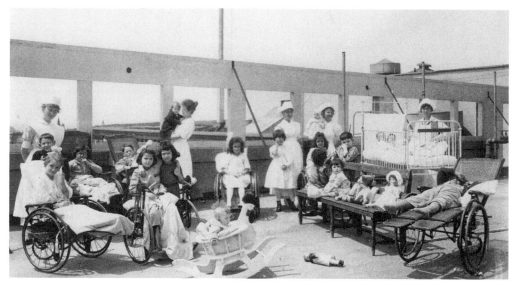

Children's Hospital, San Francisco, California, with recovering children and hospital staff on the sun roof, 1917. *Special Collections University of California Berkeley* (Call # 1989.058 1:25).

Mary Hill's graduation day, University of California Berkeley, 1915. *Special Collections University of California Berkeley* (Call # UARC ALB 19).

Pickup driving through snowbanks, circa 1929. Dr, Mary and Fred drove through similar winter storms to tend to patients' needs. *Roland Westergard Family Collection.*

Belle Butler (Mrs. Jim), friend of youthful Mary. The Butlers struck it rich in Tonapah, Nevada. Group with hoist rig at Mizpah Mine. Early 1900s. *Nevada State Museum.*

Harry Fulstone, Sr. and Annie 1934. Eleanor and Jeanne are the flower girls. *Norma Jean Hesse Wallace Collection.*

Dr. Mary and Fred with their children, Smith Vallery, 1937. *Norma Jean Hesse Wallace Collection.*

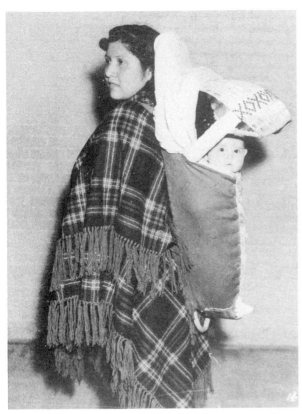

Dr. Mary did not deliver the Paiute babies, but she cared for them later. The Paiutes placed their baby in a cradleboard a few weeks after birth. The baby stayed in it most of the time until walking age. *Nevada State Museum.*

Eleanor and Jeanne Fulstone in 1950 after they became The Toni Twins. *Fulstone Family Collection.*

Annie Fulstone, known as "Grannie," mother of Fred Fulstone, Sr., circa 1940s. *Wellington Station Resort Museum.*

Fred Fulstone and Dr. Mary in a passport photograph, 1950. *Fulstone Family Collection.*

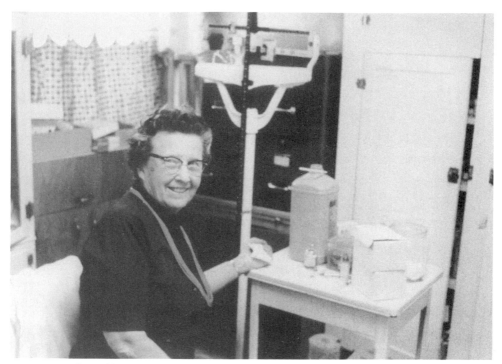

Dr. Mary in her office at the Fulstone ranch house, circa 1950. *University of Nevada Special Collections.*

Roland and daughter Tricia Westergard with pheasants from a rural Nevada hunt. Circa 1960s. *Roland Westergard Family Collection.*

Dr. Fred Anderson, Fred Fulstone, Sr. and Dr. Mary celebrating the opening of the University of Nevada Medical School, 1969. *Anton Sohn Collection.*

The Fulstone Five – Christmas 1967. Fred, Jr., Eleanor, David, Jeanne and Richard. *Fulstone Family Collection.*

Fred and Dr. Mary celebrating their 50th
wedding anniversary. Taken in the front yard
of their home on the Fulstone ranch, 1970.
Fulstone Family Collection.

Dr. Mary and Fred Sr. enjoying their granddaughters, Cynthia and Elise,
1977. *Fulstone Family Collection.*

Fulstone family portrait: Richard, Fred, Sr., David, Fred, Jr., Eleanor, Dr. Mary and Jeanne, circa 1972. *Fulstone Family Collection.*

Dr. Mary's childhood church, the Episcopal Church of Carson City, Nevada, as it has appeared since 1910. *Roland Westergard Family Collection.*

Senate

DR. MARY FULSTONE

Mr. LAXALT. Mr. President, one of the more demanding ways to make a living in rural Nevada is by accepting the heavy responsibilities of being an area physician. I use the term "area physician" because doctors are usually few and far between in the smaller communities in the State and, consequently, must shuttle long distances to care for their patients.

It requires a special kind of person to dedicate himself to a life of looking after the sick and injured in a setting which means long hours and little monetary reward when compared to urban practitioners. Lyon County is fortunate enough to have such an individual in Dr. Mary Fulstone. She has been working these past 56 years full throttle, commuting at all hours, often under very arduous conditions, to care for her patients.

A woman of her abilities could easily have opted for an easier and more lucrative practice in a larger city. Many of our young people have done just that, but Mary never left her friends.

Dr. Fulstone faithfully practices the Hippocratic oath and lives by it. She is truly concerned with helping those who need her attention and quite evidently sees past the mere market value of her skills.

In fact, Mr. President, I am probably belaboring the point here because I sincerely doubt Dr. Fulstone ever thought in terms other than being a good doctor in an area her family has lived for years. It is important, however, to recognize the wonderful and selfless career Mary has dedicated to the people of Lyon County. I am proud to have this opportunity before the U.S. Senate today.

Dr. Fulstone's hometown newspaper, the Mason Valley News, once listed the many deserving honors this woman has received as a result of her dedication to medicine and the people of Lyon County. At this time I ask unanimous consent to have that article printed in the RECORD.

There being no objection, the article was ordered to be printed in the RECORD, as follows:

DR. MARY FULSTONE HONORED BY SORORITY

At the Founder's Day Banquet on Tuesday, April 19, Phyllis Hunewill, president of Xi Alpha Beta Chapter announced that Dr. Mary Fulstone had been awarded an International Honorary Membership in Beta Sigma Phi. She also conferred the installation as Honorary Member upon Dr. Mary.

This honor is bestowed only upon distinguished women who are known internationally. Dr. Fulstone is at present the third Nevada woman to be so honored.

A tea will be held in her honor on Sunday, April 24, between 1 and 4 p.m., at Mrs. Richard Fulstone's home in Smith. Xi Alpha Beta chapter members extend an invitation to the public to attend. The chapters co-sponsoring Dr. Fulstone's honorary membership were Chi, Xi Upsilon, and Xi Alpha Eta of Yerington.

A native Nevadan, Dr. Mary Fulstone was born in Eureka. She moved to Carson City when she was four years old and remained there until her graduation from Carson High School in 1911. After receiving a BA degree from the University of California in 1915, Dr. Mary entered the University of California Medical School and obtained her MD degree in 1918. She interned at the Women's and Children's Hospital in San Francisco and then served as resident physician in internal medicine on the U.S. staff at San Francisco County Hospital. In 1920, upon her marriage to Fred M. Fulstone, Dr. Mary began her practice in Smith Valley. During the past forty-five years she has received many awards and honors.

In 1950 she was named "Nevada Mother of the Year" and she also received the Delta Zeta national award of "Woman of the Year." In 1961 the Nevada Medical Association chose her as "Doctor of the Year." She was honored for "outstanding community service by a physician" when she received the A. H. Robins award presented by Dr. Wesley Hall, president of the Nevada State Medical Association. In 1964, she received an honorary degree from the University of Nevada as "an oustanding citizen." In 1965 she was awarded the Golden Rose emblem of the Delta Zeta Sorority. This emblem is presented to fifty year members in commemoration of members who have belonged since installation at the University of California.

In addition to her private practice, Dr. Mary had been in charge of the health service for Indians in the Smith Valley, Coleville and Bridgeport areas for a number of years and has served on the Board of Directors of the Nevada State Heart Association.

Smith Valley landscape, early Spring, showing the rich, brown soil of a freshly plowed field, 2001. *Roland Westergard Family Collection.*

Smith Valley field turning green in early Spring, 2001. *Roland Westergard Family Collection.*

Fulstone ranch with barns and fence lining the pasture, 2001. *Roland Westergard Family Collection.*

Fulstone house enjoyed as a Bed and Breakfast in the 1990s-2000s, 2001. *Roland Westergard Family Collection.*

Fulstone ranch house bordered by pasture. Peace in the valley describes this scene, 2001. *Roland Westergard Family Collection.*

Lyon County Medical Center, 2001. *Roland Westergard Family Collection.*

Ranch house of Dr. Mary and Fred, Smith Valley, Nevada, 1920-1987. *Roland Westergard Family Collection.*

PARADE

Parade Chairman

1979 NEVADA DAY PARADE GRAND MARSHAL

One of Nevada's most distinguished women, Dr. Mary Fulstone of Smith Valley, heads the Nevada Day Parade this year as Grand Marshal, after accepting the nomination of the Nevada Day Committee.

Dr. Fulstone has received the honor of being named Nevada Mother of the Year, 1950; Woman of the Year by Delta Zeta, 1950; Doctor of the Year, Nevada Medical Association, 1961; Outstanding Community Service by a Physician, the A.H. Robins Award; Outstanding Citizen Award by the University of Nevada, 1964; Gold Rose Emblem of the Delta Zeta Sorority; Women's Achievement Award by the Soroptomist, 1979; name placed in the Congressional Record, April, 1976; and an award from UNR School of Medicine for Devoted Service.

Mary Hill Fulstone was born in Eureka on August 3, 1892, and moved to Carson City at the age of four and attended schools here, graduating from Carson High School in 1911. She received her B.A. degree from the University of California in 1915 and entered Medical School, obtaining he M.D. Degree in 1918.

She married Fred M. Fulstone July 16, 1919, and the following year began her practice in Smith Valley which she continues today. In addition to that private practice she has been in charge of the health services for the Indians of Smith Valley, Coleville and Bridgeport. She has served as a Director of the Nevada State Heart Association and has served on the State Board of Education for 20 years.

Her husband, Fred, was born on May 4, 1889, in Genoa and attended school in Jacks Valley and Genoa and moved to Smith Valley in 1903 from a family ranch in Carson Valley. He is still engaged in ranching where he raises hay, cattle and sheep.

He has been active in Rotary and the Walker River Irrigation District. He helped start the river irrigation in 1919 as an original member and has been on the Soil Conservation Board of Bridgeport for many years and a member of the Forest Board of Mono County.

They have five children: Fred Jr., David, Richard, and twin daughters, Jeanie and Eleanor. There are eleven grand children and two great grand children. - As Jim Sanford, President of the Mason Valley Chamber of Commerce puts it, "These two native Nevadans exemplyfy our way of life."

Nevada Day Parade Program, 1979.

VERY INTERESTING PEOPLE

SHE'S
NEVADA'S
FAVORITE
DOCTOR

A mixture of love and know-how is Mary Fulstone's prescription for successfully practicing medicine longer than any other doctor in Nevada.

For sixty-two years now, Fulstone has been on call from her huge family of patients to whom she's as devoted as to her own progeny of children, grandchildren and great-grandchildren. "Dr. Mary" is now almost ninety, but she still sees a few patients most mornings in the sunlit office of her Smith Valley ranch house sixty-five miles south of Reno.

Since 1920, Fulstone, a compact, sturdy woman, has traveled on rough country roads and over high mountain passes, at times through blinding snowstorms, to care for the Indians, ranchers and miners in her charge. In the process, she's delivered some four thousand babies and doctored five generations in several families.

Fulstone's eyes still sparkle and her mind is still alert, especially when focused on her favorite topic, her lifelong involvement with medicine. "Much of the doctoring in the early days before wonder drugs was giving moral support, staying with children when they had croup or with a pneumonia patient through the night or with mothers in labor.

"That's how I got to know the people and to become part of each family," she continues. "That is what I've always liked best about my work."

Fulstone's practice was of necessity a general one. The lack of medical facilities such as those found in larger cities required that she know how to treat a variety of maladies. "Sometimes, you did things you'd rather have had a specialist do."

A native Nevadan, Fulstone graduated near the top of her medical school class at the University of California Medical Center in San Francisco in 1918. A year later, she married Smith Valley rancher Fred Fulstone, who is still at her side today.

She's been honored as Doctor of the Year by the Nevada State Medical Association (1961), and by the University of Nevada, Reno, with its Distinguished Citizen Award (1964). This past May 8 she received the Salvation Army's seldom-given "Others Award" in recognition of her lifetime of service to her fellow man. Salud, Dr. Mary!

—Ann W. Funk

Courtesy *Pacific Southwest Airlines Magazine*, 1982.
Courtesy Maxine Rose Grosso.

Anaconda Mines, Weed Heights, Nevada, 1999. *Roland Westergard Family Collection.*

Nevada State Journal

105th Year No. 365   November 23, 1975   (UPI)

Smith Valley's 'Dr. Mary' Still Active at 83

By BRENDAN RILEY

SMITH (AP) — When Dr. Mary Fulstone began making house calls in a rattling pickup truck 55 years ago, the thorny issues physicians now face were nonexistent, but the new hassles aren't slowing her down.

"I suppose I'll practice until I die," said the 83-year old woman, who has practiced medicine longer than any other Nevada doctor — from the kitchen of her rambling ranch house in rural Smith Valley.

"Doctor Mary" is bothered by spiraling malpractice insurance rates, the way government funded health programs operate, the debate over a patient's right to die, and the new doctors' tendency to specialize instead of going into general practice.

But the hassles are overshadowed by the rewards of being a country doctor.

"I've been in on everything in these peoples' lives — the good things and the bad too. It's like being part of each family.

"I guess I should retire sometime, but I don't know when," she said at her home office. "We could use another doctor out here, and maybe when that happens, I'll start to retire myself out."

When she started her practice here in 1920, Doctor Mary caught some residents off guard. They wanted a doctor because the only other physician was in Yerington, about 20 miles away, but they weren't expecting a woman.

The ranchers and miners, however, "were glad to have a doctor here for the first time. Now these people have become like a family to me," she said.

Since then, she has seen countless patients, delivered nearly 4,000 babies, and made herself so well known that even telephone operators skip her last name when giving out her phone number.

Along with the doctoring, she raised five children of her own, took an active role in upgrading medical facilities in the area and got herself elected to the state Board of Education. She has been on that panel for 19 years.

She still keeps a full schedule, even though she has had some health problems of her own recently — resulting in operations on her back and on an eye.

Doctor Mary sees patients daily in her home, then sees more patients at the hospital and at her second office in Yerington. On a busy day, she'll handle 30 to 40 persons.

She has seen many changes in her field.

But one new trend — letting fathers into delivery rooms when their children are being born — is nothing new to her.

"It's all the fashion now," she

DR. MARY FULSTONE
... longest Nevada practice
(AP)

Doctor Mary doesn't see herself as a women's rights advocate even though she has accomplished many of the goals for which women are now pressing.

"I just never have associated myself with the women's lib movement," she said. "My way of thinking is that you get your rights, your needs met, through your own efforts and work."

"If you're busy, you're not restricted because of your sex in the practice of medicine."

But Doctor Mary's worked up about malpractice insurance rates. She's never had a malpractice judgment against her "and now I have to pay about $9,000 a year for insurance."

"That's five times what it was a few years ago."

She also questions the way government health programs are run.

"I get letters from these government agencies telling me how to treat my patients — and they've never even seen them."

The question of a patient's right to die isn't one to be settled by doctors, she feels.

"This isn't a medical question. It's what's right or what's wrong. I think God should have the final say. If there are any laws passed in this area, I'm afraid they will be abused."

Doctor Mary is worried about the lack of general practitioners such as herself too.

"There's certainly a place for them, and for the country doctor too," she said.

"It's hard work, but I love it. I love meeting people and helping them when I can," she said.

"Being a country doctor, I don't

Nevada digest

Obituaries

Smith Valley site of Fulstone service

SMITH VALLEY — A funeral for Eureka native Dr. Mary Ruth Fulstone, 95, is scheduled for 1 p.m. today at the Smith Valley High School gymnasium.

Dr. Fulstone died Wednesday at her residence.

She was born in August 1892, and was a Smith Valley resident for the past 68 years.

Dr. Fulstone was a longtime country physician, serving Smith Valley and Yerington. She was known to her patients as "Dr. Mary" and delivered more than 5,000 babies. She was named Nevada Mother of the Year in 1961, Nevada Doctor of the Year in 1963, and received the Women's Achievement Award from Soroptiist International in 1979. She served for 24 years on the Smith Valley School Board and 12 years on the Nevada Board of Education.

She was preceded in death by her husband, Fred.

Surviving are her sons, Fred Jr. and Richard, both of Smith Valley; son, David of Yerington; daughters, Jeanne Corfee of Sacramento and Eleanor Killebrew of Zephyr Cove; 12 grandchildren; and eight great-grandchildren.

Burial will be at Hillcrest Cemetery, under the direction of Freitas Funeral Home, Yerington.

A memorial is being established with the Dr. Mary Fulstone Endowment, University of Nevada School of Medicine, Reno, Nev. 89557.

Dr. Mary and Fred looking over a flock of sheep, 1979. *Norma Jean Hesse Wallace Collection.*

Headstones of Fred and May Fulstone buried, side by side, in the Hillcrest Cemetery, Smith Valley, Nevada, 2001. *Roland Westergard Family Collection.*

Headstone of Mary Hill Fulstone in the Hillcrest Cemetery, Smith Valley, Nevada. The caduceus etched on the stone represents her love of medicine, 2001. *Roland Westergard Family Collection.*

Headstone of Fred M. Fulstone in the Hillcrest Cemetery, Smith Valley, Nevada. The lamb adorning the stone represents his love of ranching, 2001. *Roland Westergard Family Collection.*

Smith Valley ranch house. Home of Dr. Mary and Fred from 1920-1987. Used as a Bed and Breakfast in the 1990s. *Roland Westergard Family Collection.*

Welcoming sign to the Dr. Mary's House Bed and Breakfast, 2001. *Roland Westergard Family Collection.*

Mary Hill graduation day portrait, 1917,
Berkeley, California. Now part of a mural in the
Lyon County Courthouse. *Roland Westergard
Family Collection.*

Plaque in the Lyon County Health Center dedicated to
Dr. Mary. *Roland Westergard Family Collection.*

A doctor's bag, used in the Lyon County area, similar to
Dr. Mary's bag. Lyon County Museum. Circa 1920s-1930s.
Roland Westergard Family Collection.

Sign from Dr. Mary's Yerington office. Currently being restored
by the Yerington Museum. Circa 2001. Roland Westergard
Family Collection.

FOND MEMORIES OF DR. MARY

The importance of Dr. Mary is seen clearly in the way she affected people. As research for this project unfolded, many who knew her made their own statements. The resulting recollections create a kaleidoscope image that in its depth and complexity completes the image of this remarkable woman.

Fond Memories is a perfect addition to Dr. Mary's life story because "People" were what made rural medicine so special for her.

List of people whose "Fond Memories" follow:

Cameron M. Batjer
Betty J. Bryan
Lucile Brown Day
Joseph Dini
Malcolm Edmiston, M.D.
Ann (Callahan) Ettinger
Janet Fischer
Richard Fulstone
John and Muriel Gamble
Shirley Giovacchini
Norma Jean Hinds Hesse

Sharon Lacey
Teresa Nesmith
Mary Nuti (Mrs. Ralph)
Basil Quilici
Adolf Rosenauer, M.D.
Roderick Sage, M.D.
Sophia Seubert
Anton Sohn, M.D.
William M. Tappan, M.D.
Robin L. Titus, M.D.

Cameron Batjer

All of my memories of Dr. Mary are fond. She was such a wonderful part of my life as I grew up and lived in Smith Valley.

In 1924 my family moved back to Smith Valley from Idaho. We lived with my grandparents, John and Christiana McVicar. My grandfather was ill and my first memory of Dr. Mary was when she came to the McVicar Ranch to care for him.

I especially remember seeing Dr. Mary driving down the narrow lane to the ranch house to care for my mother, Mabel, when my sister Naomi was born.

Most of my fond memories of Dr. Mary were when she was caring for my relatives and friends, but when I was in the second grade I became very ill with the flu and she made a house call to care for me when we lived out on the edge of the desert. I remember feeling much better just because she was there.

The education of children was always a top priority with Dr. Mary. When I was in high school Dr. Mary and Fred were two of the best supporters for our team and they drove us all over Western Nevada to our games.

Dr. Mary always had kind words of praise and encouragement to all of us. What wonderful assurance to have her as our doctor. She was a most caring, loving, remarkable human being.

Betty Bryan

Dr. Mary Fulstone was a wonderful person – doctor – friend – teacher – almost a saint.

I remember so much about her, worked with her for 30 years, she was our family M.D. forever, delivered all my grandbabies and two of my own girls.

I was her office nurse and one of my duties was cleaning. I cleaned her desk and always asked if I could throw away a cheap piece of costume jewelry she had in her top drawer.

Finally one day she said, "Betty, that's my security for a loan. I lent this person $200.00 to have a needed surgery – I'm still waiting for payment." It was still there when I left.

I know she lent many patients the money to get to Reno for further treatment.

If an OB was ready to deliver I could call her (in Smith Valley) and say I need you – she'd be there in 20 minutes. I timed her many times.

Lucile Brown Day

On April 25, 1921 in Smith Valley Dr. Mary Fulstone delivered Charles Emmett Day at the Day Ranch. He was one of the first babies delivered by Dr. Mary. Years went by and Emmett married Lucile Brown. They had three daughters, all delivered by Dr. Mary in Yerington. The girls married and in time had four children – three of them delivered by Dr. Mary. One of these children is Jenni Burr, one of the last of "Dr. Mary's Babies" born February 22, 1976, fifty-five years after Dr. Mary Fulstone delivered her *grandfather*.

One of the first Dr. Mary Babies:
Charles Emmett Day
Born April 25, 1921
Married
Lucile Brown
3 daughters born – "Dr. Mary Babies"
4 children born – 3 "Dr. Mary Babies"
the last baby- Jenni Burr
born February 22, 1976
Jenni Burr – one of the last "Dr. Mary Babies" born 55 years after
Dr. Mary delivered her grandfather
From Lucile Brown Day's "Fond Memory" of Dr. Mary

Joseph E. Dini, Jr.

I must mention a fond memory of Dr. Mary when I was injured in an automobile accident in 1949 and I went home to heal up. In the accident I had a ruptured bowel and had a Colostomy. Dr. Mary came to our home every day with her nurse Betty Brian and flushed out the Colostomy with the antibiotics and sterile solution to aid the healing process. I had Peritonitis and it was draining. It was a long process to heal up. She was so devoted, coming to our house every day tending the wound and taking care of me. I will never forget her kindness and caring of me in that bad year of 1949 when I suffered that automobile accident.

Dr. Malcolm Edmiston

Dr. Mary Fulstone lived in Smith Valley in a large old ranch house where one room was her local office for general practice. She also had an office in Yerington some 20 miles away and used the South Lyon Hospital well into her 80s. She was extremely solicitous of her patients problems, and even though getting up in years, drove to the hospital day or night to render care. This unfortunately resulted in an auto accident one night when she received significant injuries. In spite of this she continued practice, even delivering one of her own great-grandchildren.

Several surgeons from Reno operated in Yerington for many years on her carefully selected patients. She was an able assistant and followed the patients conscientiously.

Her November "staff meetings" at the ranch were attended by many physicians from Reno and included pheasant hunting on her large pastures and a Thanksgiving type meal at her home. A great party!

Ann (Callahan) Ettinger

During the years between 1954 to 1963 Dr. Mary was our family doctor. During that time she delivered all four of my children. We kept her pretty busy!

She kept office hours in Smith Valley in the mornings and came to Yerington in the afternoons. Her Yerington office was located on the side entrance of a house on Main Street. The rest of the house was occupied by, I think, one of her children and family. I remember when one of the kids or myself were ill, I would just go down to her office – no appointment was needed – and wait my turn. I don't even remember ever signing in. We just waited our turn.

I think that during the years she was our doctor, she came to our house at least three times, most always in the evening, when I or one of the children were too sick to go to the office.

Sometime during the latter part of January of 1957, Dr. Mary slipped on the ice in front of what was then the Lyon Health Center. I think she broke her ankle. Not to be slowed down by something so ridiculous as a broken bone, Dr. Mary promptly moved into the hospital, holding normal office hours from the bed in her hospital room. Dr. Mary delivered my daughter, Lynn, on February 7th of that year while sitting in a wheelchair.

Several hours before Lynn was born, Dr. Mary was in my room when she was paged to the nursery. One of her newborns was in distress. She yelled at my husband to "get me down there NOW." In total shock he grabbed the handles of the chair, pushed her out the door as fast as he could, taking hunks out of the frame as he did.

In 1962 when my oldest son was in second grade, he got what I thought was a cold. By the time I realized that it was more than this, it had turned into strep throat. He was taking a long time to recover and Dr. Mary did some blood tests. She sat me down and told me that in her opinion he had borderline rheumatic fever. She suggested I take him out of school, keep him in bed and quiet as much as I could.

I was in total shock. I had three younger children, none of whom were in school yet. It seemed like a jail sentence for all of us. I took Roy to Reno to a pediatrician for a second opinion. This specialist said to me that there was nothing wrong with this child, to get him back in school and quit worrying. I reported to Dr. Mary what he had said and she sat down next to me, grabbed my hand and said, "Ann, I have seen so many children on the edge of rheumatic fever; I have been in practice long enough to see these children grow to adults and I have seen what can sometimes happen many, many years from their illness if they are not treated. Sometimes these things take years to show any damage. Please, please keep him home and keep him quiet." Well, what can I say? I did follow her advice. It almost killed me but I took him out of school, tried to keep him up with his home-work, kept him in pajamas constantly, missed the first Nevada Day Parade of my entire life. Our prison sentence lasted from October to April of the following year. My son is now 46 years old, 6'3", was a high school All-American football player, was an All-State high school baseball player, and played two years of college football before falling in love and getting married. Was Dr. Mary right? I don't know, but I do know she wasn't wrong!!!

Janet Fischer

My first husband, Jim Fulstone, knew Dr. Mary well. In 1967 he took me to see her because I wanted my ears pierced. He called her up and she said, "Well bring her over to the house. Does she have ear-rings? Tell her to bring them." We sat at her kitchen table as she spoke about everything under the sun. She filled a pot with water and put it on the stove. I thought she was fixing tea but it was to boil the earrings. She proceeded to come at me with a long needle and cork. About then I thought I really don't need my ears pierced!! She no-ticed me squirming and reassured me it was no big deal. She just eye balled it using little dots to make sure they were even. She dropped the earrings on the floor twice before they made it to my ears. It was a whole lot more fun than if I had just gone to the jewelry store.

I have fond feelings for the Fulstones, Glen being my favorite and Barton and Eddy being right up there. I know some great stories. Someone should write a book about the whole family.

Richard N. Fulstone

One of my most memorable times growing up, as the son of Dr. Mary Fulstone, was in the evenings after dinner when she would go into the living room and sit down at the piano to play songs while we children would gather around to sing. They were special "family" moments which would happen at least once a week when I was a small boy.

I was her third son (I am sure she was hoping for a girl!) but she always used to thank me for arriving two weeks late because this gave her a wonderful "vacation" in San Francisco with her friends playing bridge and obtaining the latest medical information at U.C. San Francisco Medical School.

John and Muriel Gamble

We became acquainted with Dr. Mary Fulstone upon moving to Smith Valley where John accepted a teaching job at SVHS. This was the fall of 1947. We became personally close to her when we took our firstborn, John R., for early medical needs such as "shots." Her kind and professional attention to his needs were most comforting and built our confidence as young parents a great deal. I recall so well taking John for care to her ranch home where she had a long porch converted into an area convenient for treating patients. Her devoted care of him continued through his babyhood. She was never too occupied to fail to tend to our needs.

That acquaintance continued during John's teaching responsibilities. I recall one episode of interest. Her family had a summer home at Lake Tahoe near Round Hill. John was sponsor of the senior class at the high school. In the spring it became his task to plan and take the class on their "ditch day" as it was called then. She offered her home at the Lake and we (John, John, Jr., and I) went with the senior class for a weekend stay there to celebrate graduation activities. This was a wonderful outing for these farm youngsters as well as the Gambles.

Our association declined while we lived in Lovelock but was renewed when John began work in the State Department of Education. During his tenure as deputy and then state superintendent of schools, Dr. Mary was on the State Board of Education. It was her custom occasionally to entertain members of the board and state employees. I remember one particular occasion when we were entertained at a dinner at the top of Heavenly Ski resort when we rode the "tram" to the top. This was my first experience and the remembrance of her hospitality and generous contributions to state education department people is still fresh in our minds. Dr. Mary was a wonderful person who contributed to Nevada and the people of Nevada in so many ways. She is remembered with great fondness and admiration by all who ever associated with her. She has been missed very much over these years since she left us.

Shirley Giovacchini

I have many fond memories of Dr. Mary. She conducted her practice by not only using her medical skills but by also injecting a good deal of common sense into the equation. Dr. Mary delivered my husband, Roy, and all seventeen of his brothers and sisters in the 1920s, 1930s and 1940s. She delivered two of my children, Robert in 1963 and Lisa in 1964 – at that time I believe she was 72 years old. She said if babies were born too soon or died in infancy it was God's plan.

Dr. Mary did not make appointments – patients just went down and waited in her little waiting room until she had time to see them. My most indelible memory deals with the fact that it was possible to call her up on the telephone – explain what the problem was – and she would call a prescription to the Yerington drug store and they would send it out in the mail.

Norma Jean Hinds Hesse, Relative

There are so many memories of Dr. Mary.

Before Dr. Mary went to Smith Valley, my Grandmother Annie Fredericks Fulstone was the mid-wife in the Valley and delivered many babies. I also remember that when some of the babies grew to qualify for Old Age Assistance (something that came before Social Security) they would come to my Grandmother and have her vouch for them that she had delivered them.

Dr. Mary would never turn anyone down for lack of money, minority, cold, rain or snow and I can recall a story about an Indian Lady having trouble and Dr. Mary in her old car in the cold of the night going to deliver this child in a wickeyup. Fred, not knowing where she was, paced the floor until she returned home safe and sound and would not let her go alone for a long time.

Many times I had to have a shot for some reason or other and Dr. Mary was not the best at giving a shot, at least that was my feeling at the time. Maybe a shot by anyone else would have been just as bad.

At one point I got ring worm and someone told my mother to put iodine around the circle and that would stop it from growing. To make a long story short I woke up the next morning with an arm that looked like a map with raised mountains. Off to Dr. Mary we went and I can remember she soaked my arm in something and then popped the blisters and the next day I would go through the same thing again. As I remember this was very painful and I was sure glad when it healed.

Dr. Mary was on the school board, as was Norman Brown. One election day one of my friends thought it would be fun to go to Wellington where they were having a big pot luck lunch. Of course we had to walk but hoped that someone would come along and give a ride, as it was a five mile walk to Wellington. Jeannie and Ellie were among the delinquents and along came Dr. Mary and Norman Brown and they gave some of us a ride. There were, however, a couple boys that went home and got their car and met us in Wellington. We all decided to skip school, however, Dr. Mary told Jeannie and Ellie to get in with her and she would take them to school, Oh dear, well we told them to get out at the school gate and we would pick them up. Oh, Dear again, Dr. Mary drove them straight to the door and when we got there school had started and Jeannie and Ellie came running out the door with the principal right behind and we were all expelled until our parents wrote a note to get us back to school.

When I was eighteen, I was riding my horse. As I rode past the mail box at a pretty fast trot, the horse stopped but I went flying. I remember nothing until I woke up and there looking down at me was Dr. Mary. My mom only had to call and she came running.

Grandma went to stay with Dr. Mary and Fred for something. Maybe she went to help with the cooking, family or some other reason I do not recall, anyway Grandma wore false teeth and they just didn't fit so she mostly had them in a jar on the shelf, except when she was with or around Dr. Mary. My Grandmother made a hard candy out of vinegar it was really good, but very sticky. Grandma made vinegar candy at Dr. Mary's and came home with her teeth in a jar all stuck together with vinegar candy and she never wore them again. I think when they got stuck together she probably thought "Good, I'll just be rid of the darn things, Dr. Mary or not."

I know this is about Dr. Mary but a new thought about Fred just came to mind that is kind of funny. My Grandmother had a very dear friend, Mrs. Gage, who was around Grandma's age. Fred came to the house and told Grandma that Mrs. Gage had died. Grandma was very upset and so I drove her to Mrs. Gage's house. Grandma told me to wait in the car and she would come and get me, so here came Grandma almost on the run.

Apparently Mrs. Gage was alive and well and had answered the door. We stayed for dinner and had a good laugh. I don't remember where Fred got his information but Grandma was not happy with her son. Can you imagine the feeling at thinking your friend had died and she answers the door?

My memory of Dr. Mary: She was a great doctor, true to her profession, the Valley would have been at a great loss if Dr. Mary hadn't chosen to practice in the Valley. She was always there for anyone and everyone, rich or poor, always with confidence and a smile on her face. Family always came first and she was always there for us and I don't think that she even got paid. Not only was she a good doctor but she was a good friend to my mom and a great aunt to me, even if I think that her shots hurt.

Sharon Lacey

When arriving in Yerington in 1969 we lived at the Flying M. Ranch. The children were sick and Dr. Mary looked at them and gave them a penicillin shot. Not knowing at that time that I would have the pleasure to meet her and also work closely with her.

I pictured her as one of those doctors with a horse and buggy doing her visits to neighbors (Talk of the community when you see Dr. Mary coming through the canyon you better clear the way. I hate to venture to guess how many trips she made from Smith Valley to Yerington). She drove her car in record time.

I went to work at the hospital in 1971. At lunch she would tell her stories of her three boys and twin girls, "The Toni Twins." One day she was telling of the babies that were delivered the night before. There was a family named Olmos. When asked what she delivered will say Davis's had a boy and Almost a girl. That's how the statement was taken.

She would always have pudding for lunch. One particular day she wasn't at lunch with us and some one asked me to get them some pudding. So I went to the window and asked if I could have a dish of pudding for Dr. Mary. I almost got it but then we all started laughing and I had to tell the kitchen it was a joke.

One of the girls at work was telling the story of how Fred had been sick and he was out doing his chores. Dr. Mary tried to get him to come in and when all else failed she said, "Fred if you don't get in this house I'm going to throw rocks at your cows."

She had a knack with the kids when they were to get a shot. They got a sucker and was told now bite down. Well the shot was given and the sucker was bit in half and the pain was all gone.

She always would have a fix for you if she couldn't fix it she would make sure she got someone who could. When it came to herself and her eyes there was no good fix for her. She had contacts along with glasses and just couldn't figure out why she didn't have 20/20 vision. Her eyes were failing her and she still delivered some babies but not as many. One day she was in the hospital, she was ill. She had pills in her purse and I knew she couldn't have them so I had her granddaughter get them. I told her Dr. Mary I don't want you mad at me. She said, "I'd never get mad at you."

She never turned anyone away, always there to help. One instance I can remember real well. A little girl had an earring (pierced) stuck in her ear and it was infected and had to come out. That little girl slashed her with awful words to come out of a child's mouth. But Dr. Mary worked with her and got the earring out. Personally I'd have sent the little girl home until she cleaned up her mouth and then come back. But not Dr. Mary.

She was indeed a great lady to know. She raised her family, took care of her household duties and also did her practice. I'm truly proud to have known and worked with this great lady. She also became a great friend. Her son, David, always stops by to this day. He keeps the life of Dr. Mary through him.

Teresa Nesmith
A Beautiful Observation of our Dear Dr. Mary

One evening around 9:30 p.m. Dr. Mary got a call to go to the hospital in Yerington to see a patient. She called my husband, who is her nephew John and myself to go with her, since it was going to be longer than her regular time. I decided I would be the one to go with her since my husband had to get up early the next morning. On our way there she said, "You know when they see my car in front of the hospital, I'm going to probably have more patients calling and I will have to see them. So we will be lots longer going home than usual." We got to the hospital and she went to see her patient. Then around half an hour later the phone rang and sure enough she had other patients. She came out where I was and said, "I told you," with a big grin on her face, as much to tell me I told you so. You can't believe how happy she was helping others. So finally around three thirty in the morning we headed for Smith Valley. We talked about her patients and she said to me, "I sure do have a lot of old people that I take care of." She looked at me and laughed and said, "Gosh, what am I saying, I'm older than all of my patients."

With all of my trips with her at other times, that's the first time I saw her with a happy smile.

She liked to go to Tahoe at her home there. So lots of times I would take her and sister Jennie. She thought she would like to stay for a few days, but always got a phone call for some patient so home we would go. She was always willing, no matter how tired she was, with no regrets.

Mary Nuti

Here are some of the memories of Dr. Mary, not only of my family but of Ralph's also.

I was named not only after Dr. Mary, but also the nurse, Elizabeth Scott, who worked with her for years and whose home is where she had her office for years in Yerington, hence my name is Mary Elizabeth.

I remember the time I was about 3 or 4 years old and was very sick and Dr. Mary was trying to get me to drink a baking soda solution. I refused, but she promised me if I would drink the glass full she would give me something. After I drank it, in a couple of days she brought me a lovely bracelet with three green stones – which I still have.

Dr. Mary not only delivered myself, but she also delivered our 4 sons. Our second son, Larry, was the first baby born in the new hospital in Yerington, so she had the honor of delivering the first baby in the new hospital, 1955.

When our third son was born she said, "Mary, it's another beautiful boy" and I asked if he was all right, then said, "Why can't it be a girl?", and she said, "Oh, Mary I had three boys before getting my girls, so you still have time."

I'll never forget the time that our oldest son, Ralph, had his chin split open playing football and she stitched it up, but the next week he was back again as he split it open again during practice. After the third time I took him back she stitched it up, then used a cup from a baby respirator, lined it with cotton and taped it on his chin, then she kept punching at it and asked him, "Ralph, does that hurt?"

One morning when my dad was digging potatoes he had got off the digger to pull out the vines and his coat sleeve got caught in the power take-off and he dislocated his shoulder. Naturally he was in terrible pain and Dr. Mary just couldn't pull it back in place, so she took a tennis ball and placed in his arm pit and with her husband, Fred's, help, she got it back in place.

Another time daddy's hand was smashed in the plunger of the baler, and she wanted him to go to the hospital, but he said, "Dr. Mary you can fix it" and after working some time on it she fixed it and his hand was as good as before.

Ralph's dad, Armando, got his pointer finger on his right hand caught in a piece of equipment and Dr. Mary told him she would have to cut it off at the first joint, but Armando told her, "can't you fix it, I like to hunt and that's my trigger finger." So Dr. Mary worked on it so that he had enough of his finger so he could still go hunting.

Regardless of what time of day or night, and if she had just gotten home and in bed, when you called her, she would come to see you or you could go see her.

Even after she had stopped seeing patients, whenever I would go to visit her she would still ask me about some medical condition that one of the family had seen her about years before and wanted to know if they were still bothered by it.

Dr. Mary truly was a wonderful doctor and friend, and we mention her name often about how she treated someone or situations.

Basil Quilici

At the northwest end of Smith Valley there was a post office (managed by Mrs. Stingly) and a one-room school house. Lenore Martin Hunewill Brown was a teacher there. This area was listed on the map as Simpson, Nevada. In those days there were no identifying zip code numbers.

There was also a farm owned by Mr. Yeager. In 1929, it was leased to Angelo and Louise Quilici. Angelo had emigrated from Italy. Louise was a Mason Valley native. They were a hard working couple determined to improve their economic status. On November 27, 1929, Dr. Mary Fulstone was sent to deliver their premature baby. Without any of the amenities of a modern hospital; no running water (an artesian well), no electricity, no incubator, no central heat,

Dr. Mary helped Louise deliver a two pound baby boy, one of the smallest babies she was ever to deliver in her long obstetric career. He was placed in a shoe box lined with cotton and set on the open oven door of the kitchen wood stove. Dr. Mary insisted that her patients remain in bed for two weeks after delivery. Maria Matheus of Mason Valley came and cared for baby and mother during Louise's convalescence. The child was baptized Basilio Angelo Quilici. Dr. Mary visited the home often, watching the baby begin to thrive. She called him her Miracle Baby.

When Basil became principal of the Smith Valley Schools in 1963, they had a working relationship. Dr. Mary was serving on the Nevada State Board of Education. (She had served for many years on the Lyon County Board of Education).

Words are inadequate to describe the contributions Dr. Mary made to her community and state. To many she appeared almost as a saint.

Adolf Rosenauer, M.D.

My first contacts with Dr. Mary date back to 1957, after I had come to Reno from the University of Chicago, with two degrees in Medicine, one from the University of Innsbruck sub auspicils Austriae, and one from the University of Cincinnati, then a Neurosurgeon fully trained by US Standards. When called, I began to visit the Lyon County Hospital and on such an occasion meeting a Dr. Mary Fulstone. From this originally professional relationship grew a friendship between families, all the Fulstones and besides all those Rosenauers living in Reno also one who came over from Austria for a year. And the more I got to know Dr. Mary, the more grew my admiration for the way she handled her work and her position in life, all in such a simple straightforward matter-of-fact way and without any pretensions.

Into this time falls my first invitation to come to Smith Valley to hunt pheasants. Or this was what I originally assumed it would be only. However, the Ceremonial called for a Dinner of Fulstone Hospitality Character to follow, and then a meeting of the Staff Members, the Trustees of the Lyon County Hospital and the various Medical Consultants from Reno as they had come to be present. Complicated medical cases were discussed, hospital statistics, local Public Health matters, all things of importance to make a primary Public Institution like a hospital run beneficially, while Consultants from the nearest larger city could offer circumspection where desired. And every "Pheasant Hunt" that followed made it clearer how simply, heartfelt yet cleverly Dr. Mary had engineered that. Many a community like Yerington could only look with envy at such an idea as hers. It also kept the connection with the Medical Consultants cordially alive – when Dr. Mary needed anyone, he came, by land or by air.

On the other hand, we cannot overlook and emphasize enough the interesting fact that life had placed Dr. Mary into a time which we might consider the Classical Period of American Medicine, where for the most part an honest patient had an honest complaint to take to an honest Doctor for an honest answer. Dr. Mary's way of practicing medicine fitted perfectly into this concept. These were the years when the Professor of Neurosurgery at the University of Cincinnati was visited by some Hollywood Movie Man with the idea of filming a brain surgery, only to have this request sternly denied because the Professor felt "that Medicine was far too serious an endeavor to make it into a public spectacle or entertainment for profit." Or when a few years later, in a discussion in Smith Valley about how pseudolegal dictatings and insurance greed began to encroach upon American Medicine Dr. Mary promptly cut in: "What is all that? What are you talking about?" In all her attitudes Ethics simply came first, and thus, within the realm of her professional influence, she produced a lot of basic happiness to many people.

Yes, besides all that, she also exercised her privilege given by nature and became mother of five children and got them all raised to justifiably follow in her footsteps.

With all reason I silently dip my hat.

Roderick Sage, M.D.

Dr. Mary Fulstone being a careful and conscientious family doctor, often consulted with Reno area physicians, several of whom traveled regularly to Yerington to perform surgical and other procedures.

After a few years in my dermatologic practice, perhaps by the mid 1960s, I found myself on the receiving end of some of her skin disease referrals. In due time she might call me for an on the spot telephone consultation, some of these problems perhaps could be dealt with by phone, while others would best be treated in my office.

I felt honored to be on her "good list." This was partly an ego trip, but more importantly it was an adventure becoming friends with this revered elderly lady doctor who has single handedly held that community of Yerington-Smith Valley-Wellington together, medically speaking for the better part of 50+ years. This relationship led ultimately to the fun part.

Each fall, on a Sunday in early November, Dr. Mary's circle of physician friends and consultants, along with their families gathered at the Fulstone home on the very edge of the little hamlet of Smith, Nevada for what was ostensibly a staff meeting of the Lyon County Health Center, the hospital and clinic that served the entire area.

The meeting began shortly after dawn with a host of early arrivals fanning out over the Fulstone lands, 12 or 20 gauge shotguns poised to diminish the pheasant population of Lyon County. After 3 or 4 hours of exploring all the irrigation ditches, fence lines and soy bean fields, these lusty nimrods, feeling a certain sense of fatigue, hunger and thirst drifted back to central headquarters where more luminaries were gathering from Reno, Carson City and locally to help expand this festival.

Being a staunch advocate of the hunting "afternoon flight" I was usually one of the later arrivals, perhaps in the company of Adolf Rosenauer, Don Guisto or Chuck Lanning, when he was still with us. We would cross paths with numerous colleagues such as Bill Tappan, Mal Edmiston, John Brophy, Dave Williams, Harry Huneycutt, Ed Cantlon and many others who were there over the years.

The home of Dr. Mary and husband Fred was a substantial older, post Victorian two story frame dwelling, surrounded by mature elm, evergreen and poplar trees. To the immediate south were the several utility farm buildings – barns, garage and sheds, along with two or three hay mounds, feedlots and farm equipment. Further southeast and west were more of their pastures consisting of 50 to 200 acres. Beyond these were their neighbor's lands. These fields were all reported at times, to be teeming with pheasants or quail.

The most immediate order of business, for gun totters and newcomers alike was libation. This set the stage for the staff conference and hospital chart review along with a discussion of Lyon Health Center business, led by chief nurse Helen Barnett.

The heady aromas of the impending feast, and the sounds of the preparation lent a sense of urgency to the staff activities. Any statements or comments tended to be brief and to the point, while examination of charts was cursory but adequate.

Finally, the plate filling moment had arrived. There was always a giant, golden brown turkey with at least two different dressings, mashed sweet and white potatoes, corn, peas, beans, two or three salads, including Waldorf, fruit Jell-O and country Caesar. The piece de resistance included pumpkin, apple, mince and cherry pies, plus chocolate and spice cake.

Well now, after this repast, it was a major endeavor to shoulder the trusty 12 gauge and set out across the already exploited acres, fortunately there seemed to be a steady supply of birds to fire upon until dusk forced a halt. This event was a major family outing with most of the younger Fulstones present, including Rich and Georgia who lived a couple of miles up the road, Fred Jr., the garlic king of Smith Valley, and the beauteous twins Ellie and Jean, well known in prior years as the Toni Twins. Ellie's husband, Hugh Killebrew, the top honcho at the Heavenly Valley Ski area was usually on hand to ignite speculation about the upcoming ski season. Every now and then a bon-a-fide patient would show up needing some kind of treatment, which Dr. Mary tended to in her small treatment room.

That three hour excursion through the Fulstone farmlands was always rewarding, if not for game in the bag, then most certainly in the joy of tromping over the wide green spaces, with the hills and mountains of Smith Valley, Nevada surrounding us and the crystalline blue sky overhead. Most years the hunting was good until the autumn following that in which the Fish and Game Commission had allowed hunters to kill two hen pheasants. This depleted the brood stash and marked the finish to excellent pheasant shooting, not only in Smith Valley, but also widely across the state. In fact the bird census was so low the next year that the Fulstones purchased a truckload of chuckars so we would have something to shoot at. We hunters formed in a huge "V" from the truck parked in the field directly across the road from the ranch house. The Fulstone men released these birds, one by one. All but two of the chuckar were splattered into various degrees of disrepair; one of the survivors made his way back to the safety of the Fulstone farmyard. The other ran the gauntlet to ultimate freedom, somewhere off to the East. I always wondered if Dr. Mary might have felt a sense of chagrin about this episode. Anyway, most of us got to fire our weapons and were thankful for the opportunity.

Like most good things this lovely tradition of the yearly Lyon Hospital staff meeting – pheasant shoot – feast, wound down as Dr. Mary and Fred encountered the scythe of Father Time. I last saw them both when Fred was hospitalized in Reno with a number of disorders, the most miserable being a problem with intractable itching. Fred, while uncomfortable, accepted his situation with a certain degree of equanimity, I'm sure much more than either Dr. Mary or I would muster.

It was always a delight to work with Dr. Mary and develop an insight into the experiences of one who practiced medicine pretty much single handedly for all of those many years. She was beloved by all of the people of her community. Those of us who were honored to serve as her consultants regarded her with a degree of awe and a high level of reverence. She was very special.

Sophia Seubert

My maiden name was Sophia Bunkowski, oldest daughter of August & Henrietta. I am a real native of Smith Valley born & raised here.

Dr. Mary was a wonderful giving person. In May 1949 she let the seniors of that year graduating class go to her Lake Tahoe home at Marla Bay for 4 days for their senior sneak. Mr. John Gamble was our sponsor and his wife & little son went with us. We had a blast.

On June 30, 1949, Dr. Mary and her twin daughters, Jeanne & Eleanor who were also my friends were giving me a bridal shower which was a luncheon for over 65 people. Early on June 30, I was helping my Dad bale hay, the baler wasn't working right. Checking it he got his hand caught in the machine and mangled the top of his hand. I rushed him home and Mom called to see if Dr. Mary was home, she was and we rushed over to her office. There she was timing labor pains for a patient. Had a couple more patients very sick she was taking care of. Dr. Mary wanted to send Dad to Reno to Drs. but Dad told her you can do it. She asked me if I could help, I told her I would try. There she was with everything going on and very calm. She had everything under control.

Dr. Mary was to deliver our first baby in July 1950, but Fred and her was going with their twin daughters to Italy for the "Toni Twin Advertisement." So she didn't get to deliver our son Joe.

Two years later I was having another baby and Dr. Mary was in Yerington at her office when my labor pains got pretty hard. My husband Joe Acciari took me down to her office and she checked me and said it would be a long time yet, to go back home. We decided to stay around town for awhile, later we had to head for the hospital in a hurry and they called Dr. Mary at her office and told her to come, she came right away, as she entered the delivery room she was telling me to wait she wasn't ready, she ended up delivering our daughter in her slip, no gown.

Dr. Mary was always there when we needed her. Raising a family with sickness it was great to have her and in the same valley.

Hope you can write something about these happenings for your book. I am sure you have many interesting stories to write about Dr. Mary our dear friend and doctor.

Thank you very much,

Sincerely,

Sophia Bunkowski Acciari Seubert

P.S. It was neat to hear that your husband knew my dad.

A. P. Sohn, M.D.

In June 1968 I moved to Reno and joined the pathology group of which V.A. Salvadorini was the senior partner. Dr. Sal's group had the contract for pathology services at Lyon Health Center. Shortly after I arrived, I was assigned the responsibility of attending the staff meetings at the hospital, and Dr. Mary was always in attendance. After the luncheon meetings she usually invited me to attend hospital rounds with her and answer clinical pathology questions regarding patients. I was always impressed with her gentleness and genuine concern for the health of her patients. She explained to them that I was a consultant to the hospital and an expert thereby assuring her patients that they were getting the best of care. As I observed the patients' reactions to Dr. Mary, I could see that there was an unquestionable close bond.

On a regular basis I attended the yearly staff meeting hosted by Dr. Mary and her husband Fred at their ranch at Smith Valley. Numerous consultants from Reno attended the meeting. These included, Drs. Fred Anderson, Rod Sage, Malcolm Edmiston, Bill Tappan, John Brophy and numerous other physicians who had a high regard for Dr. Mary. There is no question in my mind that the best doctors in Reno who were on the staff of Lyon Health Center were there solely because of Dr. Mary's influence and personality. The annual meeting was always held in the fall around Thanksgiving time and it was associated with a chuckar hunt on Dr. Mary's ranch. The dinner and staff meeting were truly a country family homecoming and get together. These meetings will always have a special place in my heart with the memories of Dr. Mary.

William M. Tappan, M.D.

I'm sorry that I cannot think of a specific incident or story to tell but I would just like to say what a wonderful lady and physician Dr. Mary was. I had the privilege to know her and to associate with her in the practice of medicine for many years going back to 1953. Dr. Kenneth Maclean, Dr. Donald Guisto and I often went to Yerington to do surgery at the Lyon Health Center with Dr. Mary. We found that almost always she had already made the correct diagnosis, and she was an able surgical assistant. She showed great judgment in deciding if the surgery could be done in Yerington, or if the patient should be sent to Reno.

She was devoted to her patients and took the greatest personal interest in their well-being. She was deservedly loved by them and by the entire community. She was instrumental and a moving force in developing a very small country hospital into the fine, modern, up to date institution that it is today.

We will always remember the many good times when the consulting staff was invited to the Fulstone ranch to hunt pheasants, have a wonderful dinner at her home, and then participate in the medical staff meeting for the hospital.

I consider it a great privilege to have known Dr. Mary, and to have assisted her in the care of many of her patients.

Robin L. Titus, M.D.

Dr. Mary was truly my mentor and I have many stories to relate as one of her patients. More importantly I had the privilege of being her family physician.

For several years after my return to this valley I would stop and make a house call on Dr. Mary on my way between my office in Wellington and my office in Yerington. Initially she would spend time telling me how things were different now and how she practiced. She especially disliked the liability issues and the increasing use of specialists. Eventually, as her own health failed, she became more thankful for my advice and accepting of it.

During that time there was a nationwide crises regarding obstetrical care and I stopped doing obstetrics. It caught the attention of NBC and Connie Chung flew out and spent three days with me. I happened to have Dr. Mary in the hospital at that time so she interviewed Dr. Mary. What a special time. The show was then aired on Connie Chung's show called American Almanac. What a privilege for me to be on a national TV program with Dr. Mary.

One of the important points of the interview was how she had delivered over 5,000 babies and had never been sued, nor did she even have liability coverage. Unheard of in today's litigious society.

Dr. Mary touched my life in many ways. She literally helped open the door for women in medicine. In a conservative ranching community women were not often seen as professionals. Dr. Mary was one in every sense of the word. But equally as important she was also a wife and a mother. All roles I too try to succeed at but not nearly as wonderful as she did.

Dr. Mary also delivered my mother in April of 1925. My grandmother considered her a friend. As she became to many of her women patients.

It was a privilege to know her.

Verbal fond memories of Dr. Mary
have been transcribed for this biography.

Pink Lady	Relative
Dr. Mary's neighbors (3)	James R. Herz, M.D.
Smith Mother	David Fulstone Jr.
Doctor's Wife	Ellen Gilbert
Librarian	Nina Colvin

PINK LADY

This fond memory of Dr. Mary was told to me by a Pink Lady at Carson Tahoe Hospital.

She was visiting her mother (1970s) in Yerington when one of her small children became terribly sick. Her mother suggested calling Dr. Mary's office even though it was almost 7:00 p.m.

The worried mother was told to come right over. Dr. Mary checked the little one, diagnosed the illness, and ordered a prescription. This doctor did not care that the family was not local. (Actually they were Carson City residents). Nor did she mind that they were so late. They needed her help.

When the mother was calm, Dr. Mary sent them on their way. But, they never forgot this wonderful doctor!

As told to Dixie Westergard Summer 2001

Dr. Mary's Neighbor

A long time neighbor of Dr. Mary's told Rose Anne deChristiforo a fond memory of her. This neighbor explained that during "those years when money was scarce, many people received no bill at all from the young doctor – mother."

Interview from *Nevada Magazine*

Dr. Mary's Neighbor

Another neighbor told Rose Anne deChristiforo that "Dr. Mary would be a billionaire if she had charged for all the things she's done."

"No matter what time of the day or night, if you called she came," said this neighbor. "In snow two to three feet deep, even in the winter of 1933-34 when the snow was clear up to the top of the fence posts."

Interview for *Nevada Magazine*

Dr. Mary's Neighbor

One of Dr. Mary's neighbors remembers the young mother as "a very pretty woman with no time to dress up."

From Rose Anne deChristiforo's interview for *Nevada Magazine*.

Smith Mother

This fond memory of Dr. Mary was told to me at the Nevada Women's History Project Conference:

Her daughter's class was celebrating graduation, and a water fight began. Scoops were made of coke cans. They worked but one of the sharp, jagged cans caught Janet's daughter across the hand. Pain and bleeding pushed Janet to a quick decision. Jump in the car and drive the short distance to Dr. Mary's office. She'll know what to do.

Dr. Mary, now retired, asked them to come in. After looking at the wound, she said she could take care of this, and had everything in her office that would be needed.

Dr. Mary saved the day!

As told to Dixie Westergard, March 2001

Doctor's Wife

This fond memory was told to me at a Physician's Wives Rummage Sale:

She overheard our discussion about Dr. Mary, and stopped marking sale items to tell a Dr. Mary story. She said her husband went out to Yerington on the "courtesy staff." His services entitled their family to go to the Smith Valley Ranch for a day of hunting pheasants, picnicking and visiting. But, "Picnic" was the wrong word. A complete meal was served in the best fashion. The food was superb, and it was a wonderful social event.

All of the "courtesy staff" people appreciated Dr. Mary's efforts to show gratitude to the doctors who helped in their specialties.

As told to Dixie Westergard, Spring 2001

Librarian

A Carson City librarian said she had a fond memory of Dr. Mary, and told this story.

Her family lived in Smith Valley in the 1930s, and like many people they were having a hard time. When her sister became seriously ill they took her to Dr. Mary's office. Even after thorough examining and testing, Dr. Mary did not know what was wrong. So, she advised this family to take their child to Reno as soon as possible. But the mother said they had no money to go to Reno or to pay a doctor.

Dr. Mary said she would figure a way. The solution was for Dr. Mary to give them enough money to pay expenses, and she would loan them her car.

As told to Dixie Westergard, Summer 2001

Relative

A relative of Dr. Mary wished that Sister Seraphine from St. Mary's Hospital in Reno, Nevada was here to tell her many "fond memories" of Dr. Mary.

This relative shared one special memory attributed to sister Seraphine. St. Mary's got ready for surgery when Dr. Mary called to say she was bringing in a patient, because her diagnosis was usually right.*

Dr. Mary liked hearing these words from Sister Seraphine!

Told to Dixie Westergard, Summer 2001

In the early days of Dr. Mary's medical practice (the 1920s to 1950s) she had no x-ray, no laboratory for blood work to help with diagnosis. So, it was something of a wonder that her diagnosis was "usually right."

Nina Colvin

Roland, my husband, met Mr. and Mrs. Colvin on the Hoover/ Boulder Dam elevator during the special Bureau of Reclamation anniversary celebration. (June 2002). When Nina Colvin learned my husband was from Nevada, she asked, "Have you ever heard of Dr. Mary in Smith Valley?" Roland explained that his wife had just written a biography on Dr. Mary. Nina Colvin said, with excitement in her voice, their family had lived at Topaz for a year and Dr. Mary delivered her son. (1959). Nina Colvin lives in Winterhaven, CA.

As told to Dixie Westergard

Dr. Herz

When he spoke about Dr. Mary there was a bit of excitement filtering through years of the doctor's serious stance. He said he liked being summoned to the small hospital in Yerington.

About once a month Dr. James R. Herz, a Reno orthopedic surgeon, took care of the patient's Dr. Mary had scheduled, and flew his own airplane home to Reno.

At first he was part of Dr. Mary's "courtesy staff", then he became a friend of the family. He remembers with great fondness attending the double wedding of the twins – Eleanor and Jeanne Fulstone. This was a formal wedding and the brides wore long white gowns on July 1, 1952. The annual pheasant hunt on the Fulstone ranch and the festive food served afterward remain special memories. He had taken many photographs through the years, some of which were of Dr. Mary and her Smith Valley office. These can be seen at the University of Nevada Library's Special Collections.

As told to Dixie Westergard, January 2002

Relative

David Fulstone, Jr. had several fond memories of Dr. Mary. He liked remembering the years that she did office calls in Yerington. She worked in the yellow house and his family lived in it too. David said, with a look of tenderness on his face, that Dr. Mary ate dinner with his family many nights before driving home to Smith Valley.

He said he had gone to the 1980 Fulstone family reunion and it was great. The best party ever, though, was Fred and Dr. Mary's 50th anniversary party. Everything was the best and even the astronauts were a part of it.

David has a standard answer when asked what he thinks of some doctors. "Well, I've only had two doctors – Dr. Mary and Dr. Titus – both women and I'm still here!"

David, a Lyon County Commissioner, gave a tour to the new mural on the Yerington Courthouse wall. Dr. Mary's portrait from her Cal graduation day showed her youth and good looks. Her place in the mural is an honor earned for over sixty years of medical service in the area.

David honors Dr. Mary's memory with sweet words describing his deep devotion to her.

David is the son of Fred and Mary's son, David Sr.

As told to Dixie Westergard, 2002

Relative

Ellen Gilbert, niece of Dr. Mary and Fred, through Fred's sister, Juanita, told this cute story about the Fulstones:

Dr. Mary loved to play bridge, and she had planned to go to the lake (Tahoe) after rounds to play with friends. Fred was to pick Dr. Mary up at the Yerington Hospital, but when he arrived her car was not in its reserved space. (She had parked in another space). He assumed she had gone to the lake earlier and drove home. Dr. Mary decided to drive to the lake when Fred didn't come for her. She continued to worry about him since he was rarely late, and drove home too. No cards tonight. Miscommunication.

As told to Dixie Westergard February, 2002

BIBLIOGRAPHY

Anaconda Copper Mine Records Department
    Weed Heights, Nevada 89443 1999

Better Homes and Gardens New Family Medical Guide
    Published by Meredith Corporation
    Des Moines, Iowa 1982

Developmental Psychology Today
    Second Edition
    Random House, Inc.
    New York, New York 1975

Explosives Engineer, "Mining With Anaconda in Nevada"
by Lewis Nordyke
    November – December 1955

Fulstone, Mary Hill , M.D. Oral History – Conducted by Mary Ellen
Glass (1973-1974)
Oral History Program, University of Nevada, Reno 1980

Map of Nevada and California
    *Indicate: Smith Valley, Bridgeport, Coleville, Sweetwater

Mason Valley News, "Reflections" "Fulstones" by Cory Sanford
    Yerington, Nevada 2000
    Feb. 20, 1953, Mar. 20, 1953

Nevada Magazine – *"Dr. Mary"* by Rose Anne deChristiforo – 1982

Nevada Official Bicentennial Book – Nevada Publications Las Vegas, Nevada – 1976

Nevada State Board of Education
> Minutes of June 4, 1970
> Minutes of June 7, 1971
> Minutes of December 31, 1976

Nevada State Gazette-Journal – Ormsby County Library, References Department,
> Nevada Biographies

Nevada – the Silver State – Western States Historical Publishers, Inc., Carson City, Nevada. 1970

Pacific Southwest Airlines Magazine (In house)
> November 1982

Reno Gazette-Journal, Reno, Nevada
> September 2001

Fond Memories of Dr. Mary: Family and friends – 2001

Fulstone, Georgia, Smith Valley, Nevada, critique / edit – 2001

Tape of Speech by Dr. Mary to the Cowbelles of Smith Valley, Nevada – made available by Georgia Fulstone, Smith Valley, Nevada – 1980s

Walker River Paiutes, A Tribal History
> University of Utah
> Salt Lake City, Utah 1975

Webster's New Collegiate Dictionary
> G. & C. Merriam Company
> Springfield, Massachusetts. 1977